WALK 2.0

More Machine Quilting with Your Walking Foot

Jacquie Gering

Published in 2020 by Lucky Spool Media, LLC
www.luckyspool.com
info@luckyspool.com

Text © Jacquie Gering
Editor: Susanne Woods
Designer: Page + Pixel
Illustrator: Kari Vojtechovsky
Photographer: © Lauren Hunt

9 8 7 6 5 4 3 2 1
First Edition
Printed in China

Library of Congress Cataloging-in-Publication
Data available upon request

ISBN 978-1-940655-43-7
LSID0053

TABLE OF CONTENTS

5   Walk On

----

7   WALKING FOOT REFRESH

29   60° DESIGNS

49   SASHIKO-INSPIRED DESIGNS

69   ROTATIONAL DESIGNS

107   DESIGN VARIATIONS

133   QUILT AS DESIRED

----

174   Interval Tools A-C

175   Resources

176   Acknowledgements

Dedication

This book is dedicated
to my dad, Fred.
He's no longer with me,
but I know he's thrilled
that I am adding another
ISBN to my resumé.

WALK ON

My spirits lift and I smile inside with each email, photo, comment or Instagram tag from quilters sharing walking foot quilting accomplishments. It is hard to explain the sense of pride I feel hearing from folks who are successfully quilting the designs in *WALK* enjoying the process and experiencing the joy of finishing quilts on their home machines. After I wrote *WALK* I wondered if I had exhausted the potential of the walking foot. Could there be more?

With hours of play, trial and error, and from years of working with students in my walking foot classes, I have learned even more and I am ready to share all my new designs and ideas with you again. It is my hope that with *WALK 2.0* your quilting design toolbox will be overflowing and the process of quilting your own quilts will be smoother and more enjoyable than ever. My new designs range from simple, to challenging. Many are intricate, time intensive and require more marking and turning, but I know you can do it! I am excited for you to take the skills you learned in *WALK* and apply and stretch them as you tackle these new designs on your quilts.

WALK 2.0 also focuses on how to adapt designs and techniques to suit the machine and equipment that you have and where you quilt. Having loads of designs is appealing, but it is just as important to know which design to use, and when and what to consider when developing a quilting plan. The Quilt as Desired chapter (see page 133) provides guidance for progressing from smaller practice samples to the reality of quilting larger pieces and answering the question, "How do I know what I desire?" While *WALK 2.0* highlights and reviews the foundational skills for effective walking foot quilting, I won't go into depth on the basics I covered in *WALK*. If you are a beginner or need a refresher, I highly recommend spending some time with *WALK: Mastering Machine Quilting With Your Walking Foot,* especially the Walking Foot 101 Chapter. Learning and practicing the basics will get you on the path for growing your skills and set you up for success as you challenge yourself with the designs and techniques in *WALK 2.0.*

Finally, I want to remind you that quilting is supposed to be fun. Sometimes my lines aren't straight, intervals between lines aren't even, curves get wobbly, and I miss an intersection every once in a while. I do my best and I am proud of my work but I am not perfect and you won't be either. Perfection is the enemy of creativity, productiveness and joy. Celebrate your mistakes as learning opportunities and understand that imperfections are the marks left by the touch of your hand and ultimately reside in the soul of a handmade quilt.

I am thrilled that you are joining me again in my world of walking foot quilting. It is a place that embraces fun, resourcefulness, innovation, artistry and the joy of creating a quilt from start to finish.

WALKING FOOT REFRESH

WALKING FOOT FUNDAMENTALS

Like the other types of quilting, using a walking foot has processes and techniques that are important to master so that you can quilt with ease and achieve quality results. In this chapter, I will review these fundamentals to prepare you for incorporating the designs in the book. If you are a beginning quilter or are in need of an in-depth review, I encourage you to delve into the Walking Foot 101 chapter of *WALK*.

TECHNICAL KNOWLEDGE: The first step in establishing a solid foundation is to have a good grasp of the technical knowledge regarding the specific walking foot, machine accessories and equipment you plan to use.

Walking Foot Structure and Function

If you are an experienced walking foot quilter you probably know your walking foot or dual feed foot and its mechanism inside and out. If not, here are a few things to be aware of. If possible, use the walking foot/dual feed foot that is designed for your sewing machine. While generic walking feet are available, they tend to be less effective. Become familiar with the accessories available for your walking foot/dual feed. Many machines come with interchangeable sole plates designed for specific tasks such as quilting-in-the-ditch. Or they may have an open toe sole for better visibility around the needle.

Most dual feed machines also come with multiple foot options that can be used for quilting. Be sure to experiment with them so you will be prepared to select the best one for the type of quilting you are doing.

If available, choose a sole plate or foot that provides good visibility around the needle. An open toe foot will make it much easier to follow any marked lines and to stop at specific points on a quilt. You may need to purchase the open toe foot for your machine, so check with your dealer for availability. You'll be glad you did.

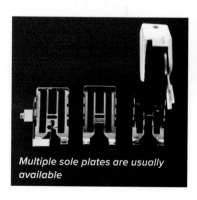

Multiple sole plates are usually available

Dual feed mechanism

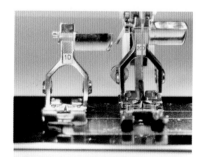

Dual feed foot options

Refer to your machine's manual to be sure that the walking foot is installed correctly or that the dual feed mechanism is engaged with a dual feed-compatible foot. It never hurts to double check! Also, make sure that the feed dogs are up and ready to work in conjunction with the walking foot or dual feed mechanism.

SEAM GUIDE

Most walking feet and dual feed mechanisms come with a seam guide or guide bar. This can be adjusted to quilt the desired interval between lines, so that only the initial line needs to be marked. Attach the guide so that it extends to the left of the walking foot.

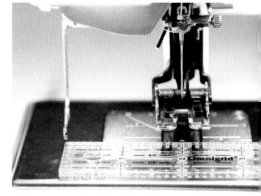

Measuring to set the interval for quilting with the seam guide.

Some seam guides are designed to fit on the right side of the foot, but this is not an optimal position for quilting since the bar is sitting in the harp of the machine and will interfere with the quilt moving through. To correct this, the bar may be installed upside down on the left. As a last resort, I suggest that my students attach the bar in the desired position on the left of the walking foot with a bit of duct tape to solve this problem. Be resourceful and creative to make your equipment work for you! If your foot doesn't come with a seam guide, they are available online or you could fashion your own with a giant paper clip and a little ingenuity. To set the interval on the seam guide, measure the desired distance from the needle in the center position to the bar before securing it in place.

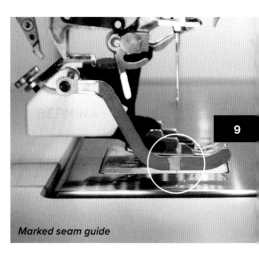

Marked seam guide

I add a mark to my seam guide that is directly across from the needle. That mark helps me keep the seam guide aligned when echoing curved lines. I do this because when quilting curves, a large portion of the bar will be off the line. To use the seam guide, align it on a marked or quilted line and then keep the seam guide aligned as you quilt.

EFNI (EDGE-OF-FOOT-TO-NEEDLE-INTERVAL)

Many of my quilts are quilted using a ½″ interval between lines. This isn't a random choice, it happens because I use the edge of my foot to echo previously quilted lines and on my walking foot, the distance from the edge of the foot to the needle in the center position is a ½″. So my EFNI (Edge-of-foot-to-needle-interval) is ½″. To find the EFNI for your machine, use a small ruler to measure from the needle in the center position to the edge of your foot for your walking foot. Typically, walking feet have either a ½″ or ⅜″ EFNI. There are a couple of machines with a ¼″ EFNI though, so be sure to measure.

Knowing the EFNI for your foot will come into play when using the edge of the foot for echo or channel quilting and for turning without marking. On some machines the needle position can be adjusted to make the EFNI larger or smaller. Be sure to check your manual to see if this is an option.

MARKINGS

When I purchased my walking foot, I took it out of the box, put it on my machine and started quilting. I didn't know that the foot had built-in features that would help me with my quilting and I was too busy getting down to business to care. My mistake! It turns out that many walking feet have echoing and turning marks etched or marked onto the foot. To see if yours has them, look for the turning marks which are the same measurement as the EFNI already identified, but are located in front of the needle on both toes of the foot. Sometimes it's not an actual mark that indicates the turning point, it may be just an indentation or an opening on the foot or even the point where the toe of the foot raises up. If your foot doesn't have these turning marks, add them. Do this by measuring the same distance as your foot's EFNI from the needle in the center position forward, then identifying that point and make a mark across both toes of the foot.

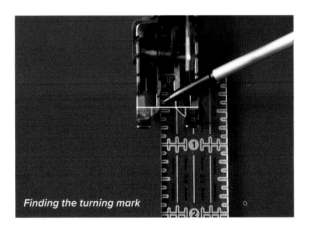

Finding the turning mark

On my BERNINA walking foot, the ½″ in front of the needle sits right where the open area of the foot ends. There is not an actual mark there, but I visualise an imaginary line across the toe at that point so I know where to align the foot and where to stop to turn at a ½″ interval.

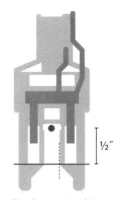

Turning mark with the line added

In addition to marks for turning, walking feet may also have marks to help echo at intervals smaller than the EFNI. For example, my walking foot has interval marks ⅛″ and ¼″ away from the needle. I use these as my reference without having to mark any more lines. Identify and mark those on your foot if you think they will be helpful to you.

Echoing marks indicated

I use fluorescent nail polish to enhance or add marks on my foot to make them easy for me to see and use during quilting. These marks may seem inconsequential at first, but after you use them for echo quilting and turning without marking, my guess is they will become as essential to your quilting process as they are to mine.

Machine

Your sewing machine is the primary tool you need to get to know for walking foot quilting. Depending on the complexity of your machine, it may have features that will enhance your quilting experience. I recommend that you read your manual from cover to cover and/or take the introductory and operational classes offered by your dealer or local quilt store to help you become familiar with the special features and operation of your machine. I didn't invest time in either of these until I figured out that my machine was controlling me rather than me being in control of it. After devoting time to learn all about my machine, I was a more confident and effective quilter.

For example, hands free features like the knee lift or presser foot hover, will be helpful when quilting point-to-point line designs or curved designs that require you to lift the presser foot for pivoting with the needle down.

Many sewing machines, even some entry level machines, have a presser foot adjustment feature. This allows the amount of pressure the walking foot or dual feed foot exerts on the quilt sandwich to be perfectly adjusted, based on the thickness of your quilt sandwich. Finding the correct pressure for your presser foot is essential to establish an even-feed and is the number one way to prevent puckers or whiskering when quilting. Many sewing machines offer hundreds of decorative stitch options that can be used for quilting and features like pattern extend, pattern combination and pattern reverse can multiply those options.

New features are added with each generation of sewing machine, so understanding and capitalizing on their capabilities will enhance your quilting experience. Become a master of your machine and you'll be well on your way to becoming a master quilter.

PROCESSES

In addition to understanding the technical knowledge built into your quilting equipment, there are several basic processes to follow before and during quilting that will support your quilting efforts.

Preparation

Basting and stabilizing are essential to a successful quilting experience. It is important to invest the time and effort into mastering this part of the preparation process. Pin, spray, or thread basting all work well for walking foot quilting. But, I prefer and recommend spray basting. I find it is easier to mark my quilts and manipulate them without the hassle of having to remove pesky pins. If you choose spray basting, remember you don't have to spray and baste in the same location. Take your top and back outside, spread them out on a tarp and spray the wrong side of both. When you have finished, fold them wrong sides together and bring them back inside to do your basting either on the floor, a table, or as I do, on the design wall. This eliminates the problems of both overspray and having to deal with fumes indoors. To protect myself, I wear a mask even when spraying outside. Be sure to follow the manufacturer's instructions from your spray baste.

After creating the quilt sandwich, heat set the spray baste by pressing both sides of the sandwich with an iron to create a flat, stable surface for quilting.

Stabilization

I avoided stabilizing my quilts for many years since I was quilting mostly edge-to-edge designs with little turning. Now that I often quilt complex designs that require more quilt manipulation, I have become a stabilization convert. Stabilization can be done in the ditch around blocks or anywhere on the quilt to define sections. It can disappear in the ditch or become part of the quilting design. Stabilization does what the name indicates. It stabilizes the quilt so that when quilting in different directions, on the bias or when quilting different designs in different locations, the quilt does not skew or warp significantly. The design and structure of the quilt determine whether I quilt in or outside of the ditch to stabilize. Figure a is the stabilization plan I used for my Lines #3 quilt. For this, I chose to stitch outside the ditch and to create eight sections to echo in.

When a design requires significant turning or manipulation like Lines #3, I recommend quilting one section at a time. After each section is completed, re-press the entire surface of the quilt sandwich to flatten out any wrinkles that were introduced as the quilt moved through the harp. Then begin marking and quilting the next section. When marking is required for the design, if the whole quilt were to be marked at once, the marked lines would also need to be pressed. Because the marks from some marking tools become permanent after heat setting, they become difficult or even impossible to remove. This is why I recommend working in sections.

Figure a

Even Feed Testing

Before beginning, it is essential to determine if your walking foot or dual feed mechanism is feeding the quilt sandwich evenly. An even feed is the key to pucker-free quilting. To determine if your machine and walking foot/dual feed foot are feeding evenly, make a sample sandwich that mimics the materials used in your quilt and conduct the even feed test.

1. Using your preferred basting method, baste a small quilt sandwich made using two 15″ muslin squares with the 17″ square of batting in between.

2. Make sure the walking foot or dual feed foot is installed correctly and that the feed dogs are up and engaged.

3. On the basted sample from Step 1, use the marker to draw one vertical and one horizontal line so that they intersect at a right angle in the center.

4. Thread the machine using the type and weight thread you typically use for quilting. Set the stitch length between 2.5 and 3.0.

5. Quilt on the vertical line from Step 3 progressing from the top to the bottom of the sample. Align the edge of the foot with the previously quilted line and quilt a second vertical line from the top to the bottom.

6. Rotate 90° and repeat Step 5 to quilt two horizontal lines.

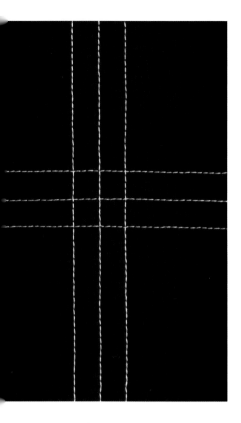

MATERIALS FOR AN EVEN FEED TEST

→ Sewing machine with the walking foot installed or the dual feed engaged

→ (2) 15″ squares of muslin fabric

→ (1) 17″ square of batting

→ Basting spray or basting pins

→ Fabric-safe marker

→ 24″ acrylic ruler

15

TROUBLESHOOTING

Inspect the intersection of the four lines carefully. Look for signs of whiskering (fig. a), rolling or puckering (fig. b).

Whiskering looks like small ripples between the lines. If there is no whiskering and the intersection of the four lines lies perfectly flat, your machine and walking foot is performing well and providing an even feed.

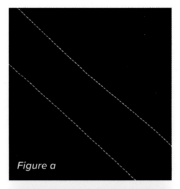

Figure a

If you find evidence of whiskering, rolling or a pucker, reduce the presser foot pressure on your machine. Too much pressure can cause the layers to move unevenly, resulting in this puckering and whiskering. Lower the presser foot pressure and quilt another set of lines at least 3″ inches away from the first intersection on your sample. Check the flatness of this intersection again and continue to adjust and retest until you achieve a flat intersection. A lower number corresponds to less pressure foot pressure. Consult your machine manual or ask your local dealer to find the pressure foot pressure adjustment on your machine.

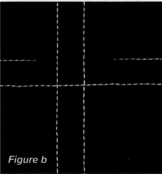

Figure b

If adjusting the presser foot pressure does not make a difference, check your walking foot to make sure it is operating correctly.

The feed dogs can be out of alignment. Sometimes a trip to the quilt shop for machine maintenance and adjustment might be in order.

A piece of lint can also affect the operation of the feed dogs, so make sure your machine is clean before beginning a new project.

The goal is to achieve an even feed so that you can quilt your project worry-free. Save your even feed test sample so that you can repeat the test before each project. It's better to test up front than to have to rip later.

16

STITCH QUALITY ANALYSIS

During the even feed test (see page 15), it is a good time to check your stitch quality too. Good stitch quality is characterized by even tension, consistent stitch length and no skipped stitches. If the stitch quality is poor, check a few things before you move to changing any settings on your machine.

1. Check the sewing machine needle. A bent, dull or incorrect thread weight/needle size match or needle type can affect stitch quality.

2. Re-thread the machine and reinstall the bobbin. The thread needs to be seated correctly in the tension discs to achieve a quality stitch.

3. Typically, having the same weight thread in the top spool and in the bobbin will help you achieve good stitch quality. If you are using a new combination of thread weights or specialty thread, the tension may need to be adjusted.

If you've checked these three things and your stitch quality is still not what you want it to be, you may need to make a tension adjustment. Look at the stitches on the top and bottom of your sandwich. If the bobbin thread is pulling up to the top of the sandwich, your top tension is too great. If there are loops on the bottom of your quilt, the bottom tension may be too high or top tension too low.

In most cases, the top tension needs to be adjusted. Sometimes, adjusting the top tension will solve lower tension problems at the same time. When adjusting either, remember that the higher numbers indicate tighter tension and lower numbers are looser tension. Change the tension by one number and quilt another line on the sample to see if the tension is balanced. Repeat until you are satisfied with the stitch quality.

If you have questions about the tension adjustment for your machine, consult your owner's manual for more guidance. I recommend that you conduct this even feed/stitch quality test before beginning each project. Investing a bit of time upfront will prevent frustration and ripping during quilting.

TIP: Use different colored threads in your test stitching so that you can identify the top and bobbin threads and easily identify tension issues.

Many quilters are hesitant to adjust the tension of the bobbin, but it is very straightforward. There is a small screw on the flat/closed side of the bobbin case. Turning the screw a tiny bit counterclockwise will loosen the bobbin tension; turning it clockwise will tighten the tension. If you are nervous about changing the bobbin tension, use a permanent marker to draw a line across from the slot before you make any adjustments. This will help you return the bobbin to its starting setting.

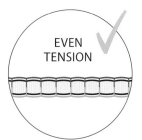

EVEN TENSION

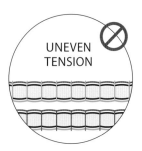

UNEVEN TENSION

Marking

I'll address the marking process for each individual design as we work through the book. But here, I wanted to share some general guidelines and recommendations. Painter's tape can be a versatile tool for marking initial lines for echoing or for defining a section on a quilt. The advantage of painter's tape is that you don't need to use several markers across a multi-colored quilt. Painter's tape is temporary, can be removed immediately and there is no worry that the mark won't come out.

Hera markers are also effective for marking initial lines. As with tape, the indentations made by the Hera markers are temporary and require no removal. I don't use one for intensive marking because the marks can be difficult to see. I recommend having multiple marking tools at your disposal. I use chalk, soap, ceramic markers, blue disappearing pens and a variety of marking pencils in white, blue and yellow depending on my project. I haven't found the ultimate marking tool that works in every situation, so by having a selection I can choose the one that works best for me at any given time.

I also have a supply of quilt pounce powder and a few applicator pads. Typically I use quilt pounce when marking with commercial stencils or stencils I've made by hand. I share the process of how to make and mark your own stencils using this powder on page 104. I love the fact that the white quilt pounce can be easily removed by ironing. Quilt pounce marking is fast and efficient.

In general, I like to use the least amount of marking possible, but we all have different levels of comfort and skill. If you want to mark full arcs rather than a set of dots, go for it. I have a set of nested circles that are perfect for marking all sizes of arcs that I use for gently curved designs.

So, do what works for you, but it is important to test marking tools for removability before marking a quilt top. I've shared information on where to purchase my favorite marking tools in the Resources on page 175.

THE BIG SIX

It's time to get to the nitty gritty of walking foot quilting: the techniques you will use to do the actual stitching of the quilting designs. You will have an opportunity to practice all of these as you work your way through the designs in this book. When you are proficient with these six techniques you will be ready to tackle any walking-foot-friendly quilting design.

→ **1.** Following marked lines

→ **2.** Echoing straight and curved lines

→ **3.** Point-to-point lines with pivoting

→ **4.** Quilting in reverse

→ **5.** Echo quilting with straight and angled turns

→ **6.** Arcs, S-Curves and Free-Form Curves

Following a Marked Line

Following a marked line (fig. a) is the easiest technique on the list. The only tricky part of this is stopping or pivoting precisely at a predetermined point.

Having an open toe foot with excellent visibility around and in front of the needle makes following a marked line a breeze.

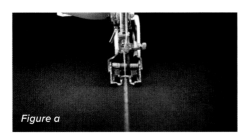

Figure a

Echoing Straight and Curved Lines

Echo quilting is one of the most-used techniques in walking foot quilting. It fills space with evenly or variably spaced lines and we will use it for the sets of parallel lines that make up the many gridded designs in this book. Echo quilting can also be used to create specialty designs like spirals and concentric shapes. Echo quilting can be accomplished using either the edge of the walking foot to quilt the edge-of-foot-to-needle-interval (see page 10) or by installing the seam guide and quilting your desired interval (see page 9).

REGISTRATION LINES

The most challenging aspect of echo quilting is keeping the lines straight. When quilting edge-to-edge echoed straight lines, I recommend using registration lines to help keep these lines vertical across the whole width of the quilt.

A registration line is a line used as a point of reference to assess the straightness of a set of quilting lines. Registration lines can be seam lines in the piecing, or a piece of tape, or a marked line set about 12″ from the initial center line on a quilt. With a larger quilt, the lines can be farther apart. As you quilt lines towards the registration line, stop halfway between the two lines and measure the distance from the last line quilted to the registration line. Take measurements at the top, middle and bottom to see if you are approaching the line evenly.

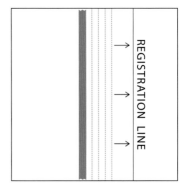

Figure b

If some correction is needed, small adjustments can be made in each subsequent line as you continue to quilt towards the registration line. The goal is to be parallel again when the quilting reaches the registration line (fig. b). When the quilting lines reach the original registration line, measure and set a new registration line and continue quilting across the quilt, measuring and making adjustments as needed. Small adjustments won't be noticeable when the quilt is finished whereas crooked lines at the edge of the quilt will be glaring.

Echoing curved lines is similar to echoing straight lines though there are a few tips that may help:

Shallow curves are easier to echo than deep ones.

The part of the walking foot that needs to keep in contact with the curve is directly across from the needle (shown here with a pin). Especially on deep curves, much of the walking foot may extend off the edge of the curve. (fig. c)

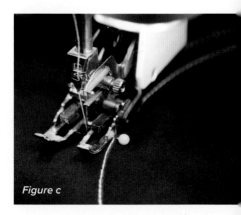

Figure c

With larger pieces you may need to have your right hand in a grip rather than a flat-handed position, so that the quilt can be maneuvered more easily. (fig. d)

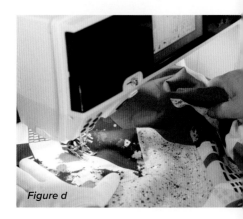

Figure d

20

CHANNEL QUILTING

Let's look in detail at the Channel Quilting process. With edge-to-edge Channel Quilting, the most common type of echo quilting, it is easiest to start at the mid-point on the top edge of the quilt, so that no more than half of the quilt top is in the harp at any one time.

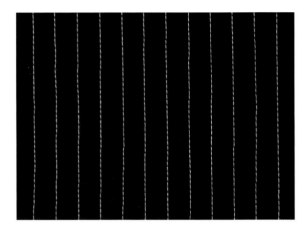

1. At the top center of the quilt, use painter's tape or draw two lines parallel to the edge of the quilt to set the first line and about 12″ to the right, the registration line. Align the edge of the foot or the seam guide on the marked line. Quilt each line top to bottom sliding the quilt back through the harp to start the next line. (fig. e)

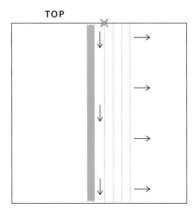

Figure e

2. Continue quilting echoed lines from top to bottom to fill in one side of the quilt, using the registration line to keep those straight lines straight. (fig. f)

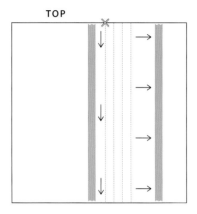

Figure f

3. Rotate the quilt 180° and repeat Steps 1 and 2 to fill in the opposite side. (fig. g)

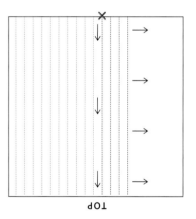

Figure g

Point-to-Point Quilting

Point-to-point lines are relatively simple if you do it with confidence. The key to success is the concept of 'where-you-look-is-where-you-quilt'. Look forward to the point you are quilting towards and trust yourself that the machine will take you there without having to look back at the needle or the foot.

Because most point-to-point quilting (fig. h) requires pivoting with the needle down, the knee lift (hands-free system) will make the quilting easier. With one available, you'll be able to lift the presser foot with a quick move of your knee, enabling you to use both hands to manage the quilt. The hover feature also supports point-to-point work as the presser foot will hover with the needle down, allowing you to pivot the quilt easily with both hands. An open toe foot will also help. The better visibility around the needle will make it easier to hit the pivot points accurately. With practice, you will be able to quilt longer and longer lines, point-to-point, without having to mark them.

Reverse Quilting

The majority of walking foot quilting is done quilting forward, hence my favorite phrase 'forward-motion' instead of 'free-motion' quilting. Occasionally, reverse quilting (fig. i) comes into play offering new designs and reducing the need to turn the quilt frequently.

You need to understand how your machine works in reverse and to keep the length of quilting relatively short. Because of the reduced visibility behind the needle, the quilt is more difficult to control. Typically, reverse quilting requires pivoting, so using a knee lift or hover feature will be very helpful here too.

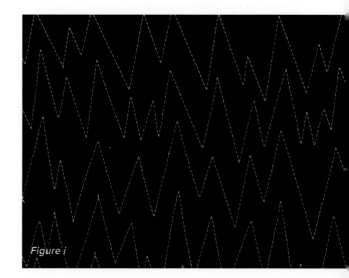

Figure i

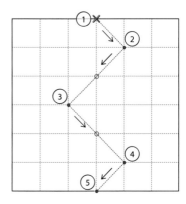

Figure h

Echo Quilting with Turning

Echo quilting can be done with straight lines, curves or with turning. If using your EFNI (see page 10) you can use the edge of the walking foot to make turns without marking. To do this, mark across the toe of your foot the same distance forward from the needle as the EFNI for your walking foot. This mark will prompt you to stop and drop the needle to prepare to turn. See page 11 for marking instructions.

RIGHT ANGLE TURNS

When approaching a line where you want to turn, slow down and stop when the mark on your foot hits the line. If you've marked your foot accurately, when you pivot, the edge of your foot will be aligned at the correct interval and you should be ready to quilt on. Adjust your mark if needed to get an accurate turn.

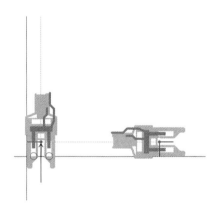

Stop with the needle down when the mark on the foot that is the EFNI in front of the needle reaches the marked line. Pivot and the foot should be aligned with the marked line and ready to quilt a perfect 90° angle.

OTHER ANGLED TURNS

When approaching a line from an angle, one of the toes of the foot is going to reach the line first. Slow down as you approach and watch that toe. Stop with the needle down when the mark in the center of that toe first hits the line. It may take some experimenting to find the right point at which to stop, but once you know, you can repeat it for each turn you make. Pivot to check the alignment of the foot and adjust your mark if necessary. After pivoting, the edge of the foot should be aligned at the correct interval and you should be ready to quilt on.

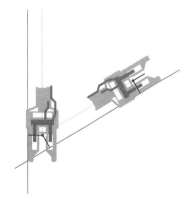

Notice how the toe on the right reaches the line first. Even though the line that is the correct interval forward from the needle runs across the whole foot, the turn point marked by the dot is in the middle of the right toe.

Quilting Arcs and S-Curves

Depending on how you mark the curves, quilt arcs and S-Curves on the marked lines, with a variation of the point-to-point process, or free-form. S-Curves feel almost continuous, while arcs feel choppier due to the frequent pivoting. Free-form quilting is so freeing!

MARKED CURVES

Feel free to fully mark any of the curved designs in the book. Sometimes it is less stressful to invest time up front in marking to make the quilting easier.

S-Curves (fig. j) are made up of arcs turned in opposite directions and stacked on top of each other. If possible, quilt in a continuous S-Curve motion to reduce the amount of pivoting required. Stop at the top or bottom of each arc to rest, breathe and adjust the quilt. If the design doesn't offer an S-Curve option, quilt on the marked arc (fig. k) and stop with the needle down, then pivot to begin each new arc. Again, each time you stop with the needle down is a good opportunity to adjust the quilt.

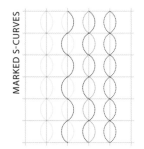

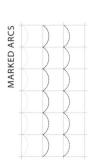

Figure j

Figure k

POINT-TO-POINT VARIATION

For many of the curved designs in the book, I recommend using a dot to mark the location of the deepest part of a curve. With a marked dot, I can use a variation of the point-to-point line method (see page 22) and the 'where-you-look-is-where-you-quilt' concept to quilt curves using minimal marking (figs. l & m). In fact, I'll let you in on a little secret: because of the amount of practice I have had with this method, I no longer mark at all! I've trained my eye to look to where the deepest part of the curve is located. The key to this method is to look at the dot and wrap around it rather than quilt directly towards it. Wrapping around results in a curve rather than a line.

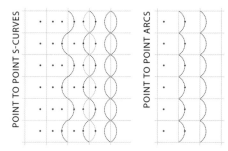

Figure l

Figure m

As with point-to-point lines, it is essential to trust yourself and look forward to the marked dot and intersections. Then quilt in an S-Curve motion if possible to reduce the amount of pivoting required. Moving the quilt sandwich creates the curve, so gripping the quilt with your right hand may help you move it more easily than with a flat-handed position.

FREE-FORM CURVES

S-Curves can be quilted without any marking at all. The easiest curves to quilt using this method are shallow curves, as in the Pinwheels design. (fig. n)

Notice how those curves have a depth of less than ¼″ which means very little movement of the whole quilt sandwich is needed to produce those curves.

While some control is necessary to make sure the tops and bottoms of the curves cross grid lines, remember to apply the 'where-you-look-is-where-you-quilt' concept to keep the curves placed where you want them to be. Without the grid, free-form curves can move randomly and flow wherever you want them to go.

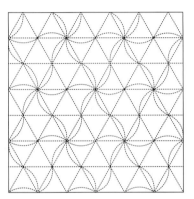

Figure n

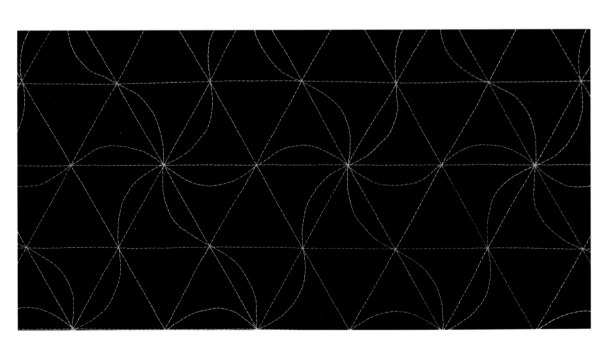

SEND OFF

Practice

Practice is imperative, and with each quilt you make, your skills will improve and your confidence will grow. A word of advice about learning and using new designs though: start small and work your way to larger quilts. If it is your first time trying Rotational Designs (see page 69), make a set of pillows or use the designs on a wall hanging before you jump to using the designs on larger quilts. Practicing on smaller pieces will allow you to become familiar with the skills required for a new design, will help you build muscle memory and, of course, will inspire confidence. Small successes are the foundation for big successes.

Walk Don't Run

I said this in *WALK* and I'm saying it again for 2.0. Walk, don't run.

It's called a walking foot for a reason. Find a rhythm as you quilt, but try not to be a speed demon. I know we're all in a hurry to finish our quilts and I admit, patience is not one of my strengths. I've been a speed demon too. But I always regret it. My quilting is not as straight and my stitch quality and evenness is never as good when I go quickly. Take your time, relax your shoulders, enjoy and savor every stitch.

" There are a whole new set
of designs to share based on
these magical 60° lines.

60° DESIGNS

In WALK, I share examples and techniques for grid or crosshatch quilting. I suggest crosshatching with lines at different angles and shared several options, but I neglected to explore the potential of a grid composed of 60° lines. Turns out there is a whole new set of designs to share using this grid: diamonds, triangles, simple or complex grids and other intriguing designs that are shared based on these magical 60° lines.

60° DIAMOND CROSSHATCH

This grid is the foundation for all the designs in this chapter.

1. With the quilt top basted and pressed, align the 60° line of a ruler along the bottom edge of the quilt top so that there is about one half of the quilt top on either side of the ruler (fig. b). The ruler will now be angled at 60°.

2. Using a fabric-safe marker (see page 18), draw a line along the edge of the ruler.

3. Extend the line to the top of the quilt.

4. Reposition the ruler so it points in the crosswise direction, keeping the 60° line aligned with the bottom of the quilt. Again, there should be about one half of the quilt top on either side of the ruler.

5. Repeat Steps 2-3 to mark in the crosswise direction. (fig. c)

6. Install the seam guide that comes with your walking foot or dual feed foot.

7. Determine the desired interval between the quilting lines. Measure this distance from the needle to the seam guide bar and tighten the bar in place. Wider intervals will appear more like a diamond motif whereas closer ones create an overall

----
TIP: Most 6″ x 24″ acrylic rulers have lines printed on them indicating angles printed: 30°, 45° and 60° are typical. If your ruler doesn't have all of those lines, I suggest upgrading. These rulers are extremely useful for marking. I've come across a few rulers that are incorrectly marked. Check to see that your angle measures 60° by comparing it with Figure a.

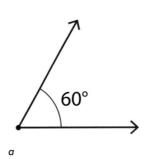

a

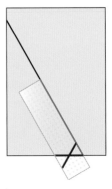

b

diamond texture. If you are quilting a variation in this chapter, wider intervals will allow room for additional design elements. If you are unsure about which interval to use, either draw or quilt a test sample. My sample uses a 1½″ interval.

8. Align the seam guide with the left leaning 60° marked line and echo quilt lines across one half of the quilt using the interval established in Step 7. **(fig. d)**

9. Rotate the quilt 180° and repeat Step 8 to fill the opposite side. **(fig. e)**

10. Repeat Steps 4-5 with the previously marked opposite angled line to complete the grid. **(fig. f)**

TIP: If you don't have a seam guide, you can fashion one from a giant paper clip or buy a generic seam guide (Resources page 175) and duct tape it to your foot. Install the guide on the left side of the walking foot if possible. Before making any modifications to your machine, be sure to check with your dealer so that the warranty is not compromised.

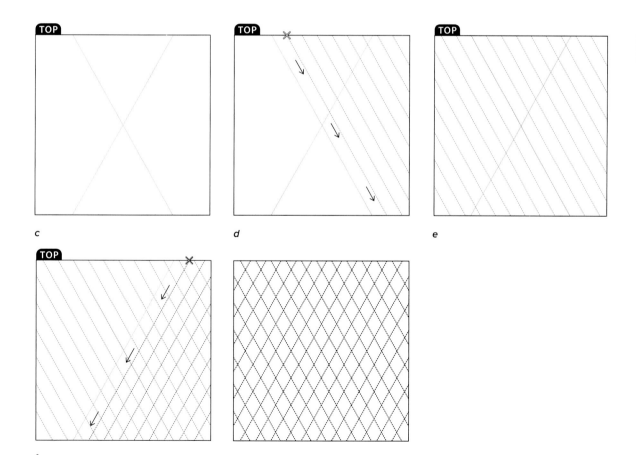

c

d

e

f

EQUILATERAL TRIANGLE GRID

The Equilateral Triangle grid is the second foundational design for this chapter. The three equal sides of this triangle create the perfect structure for intricate symmetrical designs with the addition of point-to-point lines or gentle curves. The lines required to create the Equilateral Triangle grid can be quilted using the seam guide or they may be quilted point-to-point without using the guide, which I find to be easier and more accurate. If you do too, remember the concept is 'where-you-look-is-where-you-quilt'. By looking to the next intersection, you will quilt a straight line from one intersection to the next.

I find when I quilt point-to-point, I hit the intersections accurately whereas when I use the seam guide method, if there is any variation in my quilting of the foundational Diamond Crosshatch, I don't have as much flexibility to adjust my line to create a clean intersection. I also tend to want to look away from the guide to check the intersections as I'm quilting and it is impossible to look at two places at once no matter how hard I try. To have the lines coming together perfectly at the intersections, is more important to me than having accurate intervals between the lines. Try both methods and decide on the one that works best for you.

TIP: Quilting point-to-point involves trusting yourself to look forward to the point you are quilting towards. Keep your eye fixed on that point and you'll be able to quilt a straight line to it. You may be tempted to look back at the foot or the needle, but resist that urge and try your best to look forward. Stop with the needle down when you reach the point, look forward to the next point and continue quilting.

The Point-to-Point Method

1. For either method, first quilt a Diamond Crosshatch (see page 30) using your desired interval. (fig. a)

2. Rotate the quilted Diamond Crosshatch 90°. Starting at the center, indicated here by the red X, quilt from point-to-point across the quilt, dividing the diamonds into triangles.

3. Repeat with the next set of diamonds and proceed across the quilt. (fig. b)

4. Rotate the quilt 180° and repeat Steps 2-3 to complete the opposite side.

The Seam Guide Method

1. For either method, first quilt a Diamond Crosshatch (see page 30) using your desired interval. (fig. a)

2. Rotate the quilted Diamond Crosshatch 90°. Align the needle with the upper tip of the center diamond indicated here by the red X. Make sure the seam guide is aligned with the previous row of intersections indicated here by the red line. Keep the seam guide aligned on the line of intersections as you quilt and divide the diamonds into triangles. (fig. c)

3. Align the seam guide with the previously quilted line and proceed across the quilt dividing each line of diamonds into triangles.

4. Rotate the quilt 180° and repeat Steps 2-3 to complete the design.

a

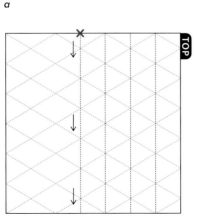

b

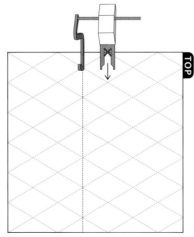

c

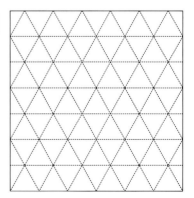

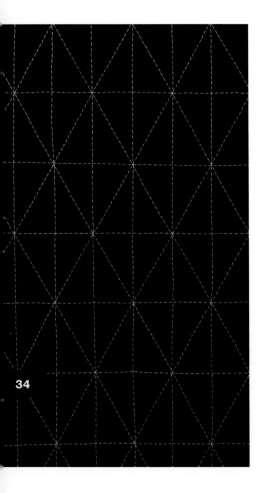

Divided Diamonds

Adding one additional set of parallel lines to the Equilateral Triangle Grid (see page 32) creates the Divided Diamonds design. The diamonds in the foundational grid will be divided into four sections creating a moderate level of complexity and a lovely texture. The Divided Diamond design is made up of four sets of parallel lines, so while it is simple to quilt, it is a time intensive design.

1. Referring to page 32, quilt an Equilateral Triangle using your desired interval. My sample is quilted using a 1½″ interval. (fig. a)

2. Starting at the top on the center X, use either the seam guide or point-to-point method (see page 21) to quilt vertical lines through the center of each line of diamonds in the grid. Quilt from the center to the right side of the quilt. (fig. b)

3. Rotate the quilt 180° and complete the design.

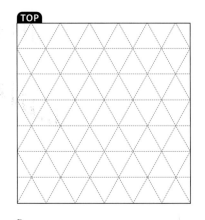

a

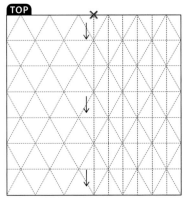

b

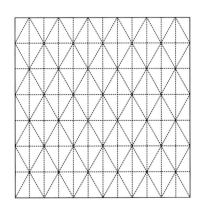

Argyle

Argyle is a variation of the Diamond Crosshatch (see page 30) that is achieved by using two different thread weights and colors. This is a perfect design if you are looking for a quirky and fun quilting motif.

1. Using a heavyweight thread (I recommend 28-weight) in color #1, quilt the Diamond Crosshatch using a 1½″ interval.

2. Change to a lightweight thread (I recommend 40- or 50-weight) in color #2. Draw a line half way between two already quilted lines roughly in the center of the quilt using a fabric-safe marker. Starting at the red X, quilt along that marked line. Align the seam guide with the quilted line and quilt a line between the next two previously quilted lines. (fig. a)

3. Move the quilt top to align the seam guide to the next lightweight line and continue quilting across the quilt. (fig. b)

4. Rotate the quilt 180° and complete the lightweight lines on the opposite side.

5. Repeat Steps 2-4 by drawing a line starting at the green X in the opposite direction to complete the design.

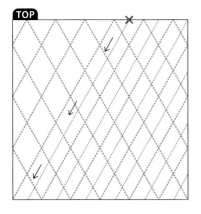

a

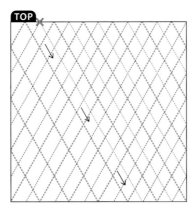

b

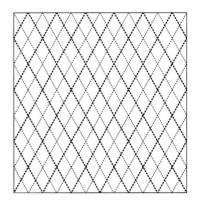

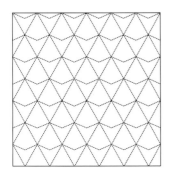

Fish Scales

Fish Scales is a 60° Diamond Crosshatch in which a gentle scallop is added. It requires a stop and a slight pivot to quilt from scallop-to-scallop. Fish Scales is beautiful when quilted on a small scale, for example, a 1″ grid and ¼″ scallop depth. This is more time consuming, but worth it for a special project.

1. Quilt a 60° Diamond Crosshatch (see page 30). Using the edge of a small circle template or a small plate or mug, mark shallow arcs through the middle of the diamonds. (fig. a)

2. Rotate the quilt 90° and begin quilting along the marked lines from Step 1. Drop the needle at the red X. Aim down the arc and quilt to the next intersection. (fig. b)

3. Once at the intersection, stop with the needle down. Use the knee lift or raise the presser foot and pivot slightly. Aim for the next dot to quilt the next scallop. Continue quilting scallops on each line of triangles across the whole width of the quilt or to the edge of the quilted area.

TIP Use point-to-point lines creating a shallow 'V' instead of curves for scallops to yield a different look.

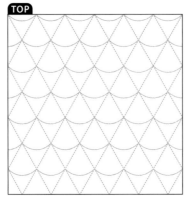

a

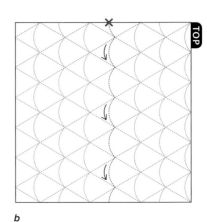

b

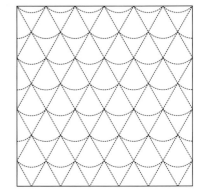

Morocco

How about a little international flavor? This is fairly simple to quilt keeping the S-Curves to ⅛″ to ¼″, but the smaller the grid, the more challenging the just-barely-curves will be. Though you are welcome to mark them, I encourage you to quilt the curves without marking. The charm of Morocco is that the curves are not perfect, creating the look and feel of Moroccan tile. My sample grid is quilted at a 2½″ interval.

1. Quilt a 60° Diamond Crosshatch (see page 30).

2. If desired, mark the halfway point between each grid intersection at the point where the S-Curve changes direction.

3. Starting at the red X, quilt S-Curves between the intersections on both sides of the grid lines. Start the curve towards the inside of the diamond on each line. (fig. a)

4. Rotate the quilt 180° and repeat Step 3 to complete the S-Curves on the remaining lines in the first direction.

5. Rotate the quilt 90° and repeat Steps 3-4 for the grid lines in the opposite direction (fig. b). Again, remember to start the curve towards the inside of the diamond.

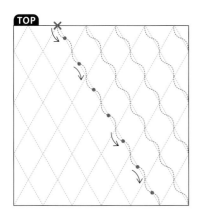

a

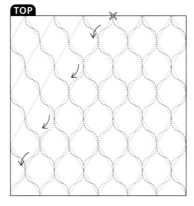

b

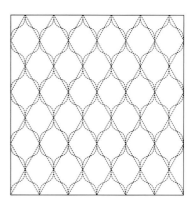

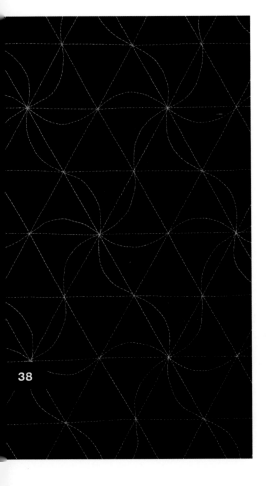

Pinwheels

The Equilateral Triangle Grid is the foundation for the Pinwheels design. This design is reasonably easy and quick to quilt since the gentle curves are only added to one side of every other line in the grid. The key to this design is making sure that the curves are consistently quilted on the correct side of the line so that they form those beautiful Pinwheels. My sample is quilted using a 2″ grid.

1. Quilt the Equilateral Triangle Grid (see page 32).

2. Starting at roughly the top center of the grid, select a left leaning 60° line. On that line, quilt gentle S-Curves from intersection to intersection with the depth of the curve about ¼″ away from the grid line. If you need more of a guide for the curve, mark a dot ¼″ away from the center of the line or mark the full curve starting on the right side of the line and move down the line as shown in Figure a. The edge of my 3″ diameter circle template works well for marking on a 2″ grid.

3. Quilt every other left-leaning line in the same way, making sure to quilt the curve beginning on the same side of the line for the first curve on each.

4. Rotate the quilt 180° and repeat Step 3 to finish the first set of lines. **(fig. b)**

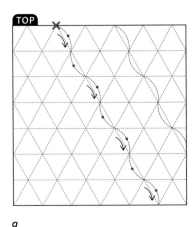

a

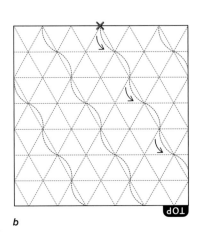

b

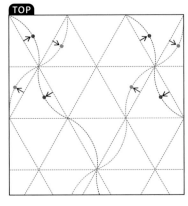

c (detail)

5. Locate a right leaning 60° line that intersects an already quilted line. Repeat Steps 2-4 being sure to keep the curve on the same side of the grid line and to only quilt on every other line. **(fig. c)**

6. Rotate the quilt 90° and locate a vertical line near the center of the quilt on which two sets of curvy lines already intersect. Start quilting at that line. It is important that the curved lines which form the Pinwheels are on the correct side of the line. Look carefully at the detail of the Pinwheel in Figure d to remind yourself how to form the Pinwheel shape. **(fig. d)**

7. Quilt the curves on the vertical line from Step 6 working from intersection to intersection to complete the first vertical line of S-Curves still starting on the same side of the grid line as in Steps 2 and 5.

8. Quilt every other line to the right of that line with the curves starting in the opposite direction for each line. **(fig. e)**

9. Rotate the quilt 180° and quilt curves from intersection to intersection on every other line to complete the design. Make sure the curves are in the correct position to form those Pinwheels!

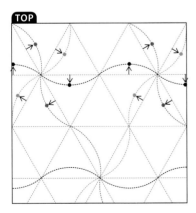

d (detail)

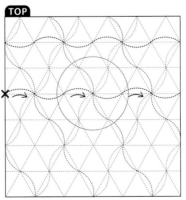

e

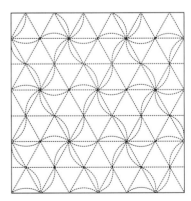

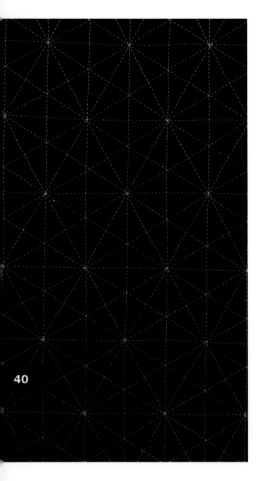

The Six Set Grid

The Six Set Grid has become my new favorite design. It is intense, time consuming and simply fabulous when all those lines come together at each intersection. It begins as the 60° Diamond Crosshatch, then it becomes an Equilateral Triangle Grid, then Divided Diamonds and finally, two additional sets of parallel lines are added to create this complex grid. When the design is finished, each equilateral triangle will be subdivided by three lines as shown here in Figure a.

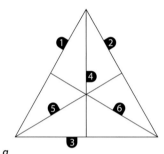

a

If you get lost in the design, use the anchor triangle and look at it and you'll know right away what is left to quilt. Get ready for a marathon of quilting.

Are you up for it?

1. Quilt the Divided Diamond design (see page 34).

2. Find an equilateral triangle roughly in the center of the quilted design and outline it or circle it with a fabric-safe marker. This is your anchor triangle (fig. b). With the quilting you have done up to this point, there should already be one line quilted within the anchor triangle. Next, we will add the other two lines.

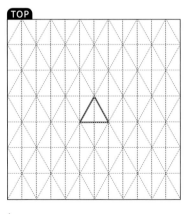

b

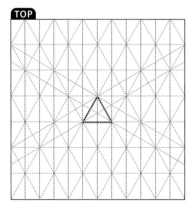

c

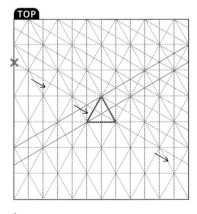

d

3. Mark a line from the right apex of the anchor triangle to the midpoint of the opposite side going through the middle of the triangle. Extend that line in both directions across the quilt as shown in Figure c, still going through the center of the triangles. Draw a second line parallel to the first line (fig c). Use these two drawn lines to set the interval for your seam guide.

4. Repeat Step 3 and mark the two lines starting on the left apex of the anchor triangle before beginning any quilting. With so many lines in this design, it is easy to get confused even with the help of the anchor triangle. Use the Seam Guide Method (see page 33) for the final two sets of lines in this quilt. I actually use the Point-to-Point Method, but it can get confusing until you have built up experience with this design.

5. Quilt on both drawn lines from Step 4 in one direction and then use the seam guide to echo quilt another set of lines across the quilt. (fig. d)

6. Rotate the quilt 180° to complete the opposite side.

7. Rotate the quilt 90° and repeat Steps 5-6 in the opposite direction to complete the Six Set Grid. (fig. e)

TIP: When quilting these two sets of lines, you will be dividing a row of diamonds in half each time. Look for the diamonds as you quilt. Finding them will help you quilt point-to-point from the top to the bottom of each. When quilting the last set of lines, each diamond will have two intersections inside which are good intermediate points to reference as you quilt. (fig. f)

41

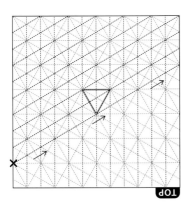

e

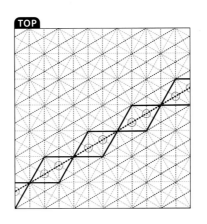

f

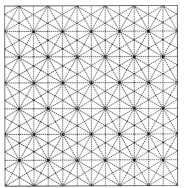

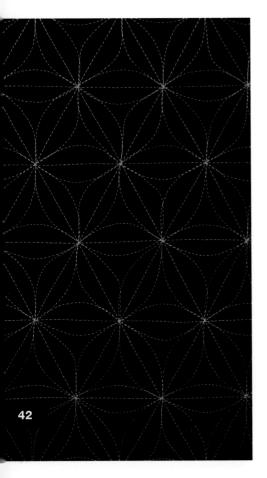

Flowers in Circles

Flowers in Circles is a beautiful design that capitalizes on the three equal sides of the Equilateral Triangle Grid that serves as the foundation for this design. This is a time-consuming design. It requires quilting a gentle S-Curve pattern on both sides of each of the three grid lines of the equilateral triangle grid. Be sure to test the interval you choose for this design. With smaller intervals between lines, it may be more challenging to quilt the curves even though they are gentle. It is also important to reduce the depth of the curve with a smaller grid. My sample is quilted with a 2″ interval and a scant ½″ depth to the curve. When I quilt Flowers in Circles, I like to break it up into steps that I tackle one day at a time. I quilt the equilateral triangle grid on the first day and then I take one day to do the S-Curve marking. Finally, I use another day or so to quilt the S-Curves in the three directions. As I said, this is a time consuming design, but anything that is this pretty is worth it, and I find breaking it into parts makes the quilting feel more manageable. Decide for yourself which quilts are worth this kind of investment. Take your time and enjoy the process. You'll be glad you did!

TIP: Try creating a marking template by cutting a 1″ wide rectangle the length of a grid line. Fold the rectangle in half lengthwise and cut a gentle curve from top to bottom. Use the resulting pod shape to mark this design.

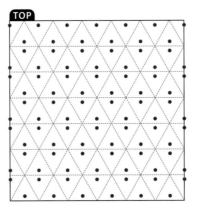

a

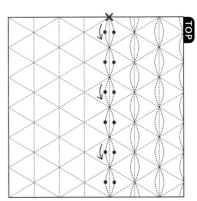

b

1. Quilt an Equilateral Triangle Grid (see page 32).

2. Using a fabric-safe marker, mark dots ½″ above and below the center point of each triangle base on the horizontal lines of the grid. Alternatively, mark a pod shape centered on each grid line if preferred. **(fig. a)**

3. Rotate the quilt 90°. Slide the quilt back through the harp and starting in the opposite direction quilt another S-Curve pattern down the line to complete the pod shape. Use the dot or traced curve to establish the depth of the curve and keep it consistent. **(fig. b)**

4. Repeat Step 3 to quilt the curves on the remainder of the marked lines to fill in the first side of the quilt.

5. Rotate the quilt 180° and finish quilting the curves on the opposite side.

6. Repeat Steps 2-5 to mark and quilt the set of left leaning lines. **(fig. c)**

7. Repeat Steps 2-5 again to quilt the set of right leaning lines on the third side of the triangle to complete the design. **(fig. d)**

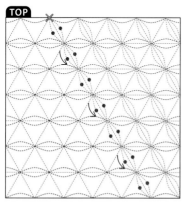

c

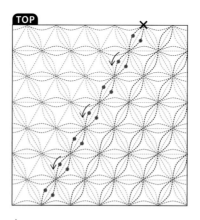

d

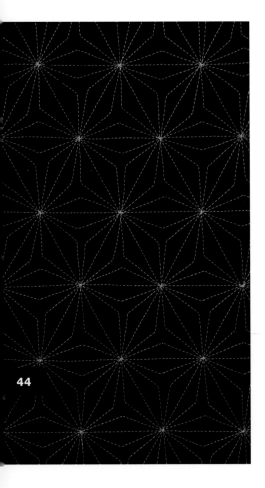

Point-to-Point Flowers in Circles

I love the Flowers in Circles Design (see page 42). It is full of movement and the pod shapes form a secondary design of beautiful circular shapes. By changing those curves to point-to-point lines, the design transforms into something totally different yet still intricate and stunningly beautiful. If you have them, use the knee lift or hover feature of your machine to make pivoting easier for this design.

1. Repeat Steps 1-2 from page 43.

2. Repeat Steps 3-7 from page 43, this time, quilting point-to-point straight lines connecting each mark instead of S-Curves. (figs. a-c)

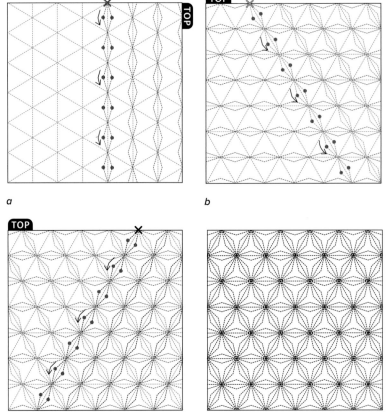

a

b

c

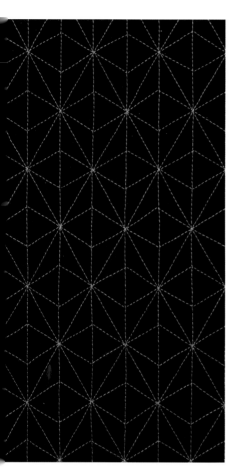

Diamonds in Diamonds

The Diamonds in Diamonds Design is a simple point-to-point design that floats a small diamond within a larger diamond. I love the fact that it looks complex, but is very easy to mark and quilt. Again, use the knee lift or hover feature on your machine if you have them to help make the point-to-point pivoting for this design easier.

1. Quilt the Diamond Crosshatch on page 30. I used a 2″ interval for my sample. Start at the top center and quilt a vertical line through each row of diamonds. Rotate the quilt 180° and repeat to complete the opposite side of the quilt.

2. On each vertical line, use a fabric-safe marker to mark ½″ away from either side of the midpoint of each grid line. **(fig. a)**

3. Rotate the quilt 90° and quilt point-to-point in a zigzag pattern down the line. Slide the quilt back through the harp and repeat the process to complete the opposite side forming diamonds down the entire line of the grid. **(fig. b)**

4. Repeat Step 3 for all of the vertical lines to complete the first side of the quilt.

5. Rotate the quilt 180° and repeat Steps 3-4 to complete the design.

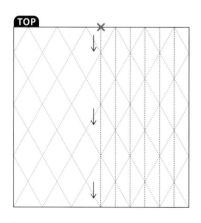

a

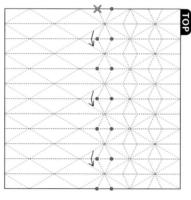

b

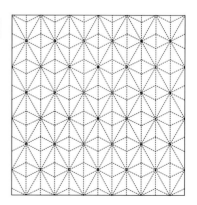

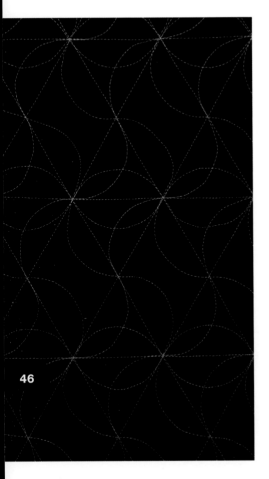

Waving Diamonds

Recently, I was working on some rotational designs using a sliced curve shape and was experimenting with overlapping designs. With one version, the design you see on the left appeared and Waving Diamonds was born. My sample is quilted using a 2½″ grid and a 1″ depth of curve. This 1″ depth of curve is challenging to quilt, but I wanted to push myself. For your first attempt, I would recommend marking a shallower curve.

1. Quilt the 60° Diamond Crosshatch (see page 30) using a 2½″ interval.

2. Rotate the quilt 90°. Start roughly in the center of the quilt and quilt vertical lines to divide every other diamond into equilateral triangles.

3. Rotate the quilt 180° and repeat Step 2 to complete the opposite side. (fig. a)

4. Mark dots ½″ away from both sides of the midpoint of each grid line on all the vertical lines. Feel free to mark the full curve if you wish.

TIP: Dots can be marked at ¼″, ½″, or 1″ away to reduce or increase the difficulty of the design and create a different look. Just be sure to keep the marked interval consistent throughout the design once you have decided on your interval.

a

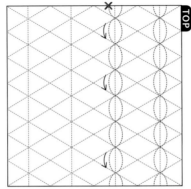

b

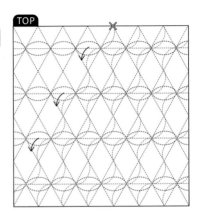

c

5. Quilt in an S-Curve pattern down both sides of the vertical lines quilted in Step 2 using the dots to guide the depth of the curve or following the marked curves. **(fig. b)**

6. Rotate the quilt 180° and repeat Step 5 to complete the opposite side.

7. Rotate the quilt 90°. Mark dots ½″ away from the mid point or mark the curves on the right-leaning 60° lines, but only mark a single S-Curve this time. Quilt the curves in each, beginning in the same direction and crossing over the straight lines in a pinwheel fashion. Go from one side of the line to the other using the marks or dots to guide the depth of the curves, indicated here in green. **(fig. c)**

8. Rotate the quilt 180° and repeat Step 7 to complete the opposite side, keeping the curves on the same side of the line in each row.

9. Repeat Steps 7-8 on the left leaning lines to complete the design. **(fig. d)**

SEND OFF

It is funny how giddy I get with the thought of a 60° grid. I believe I've only scratched the surface of the potential it has as the foundation for many more designs that add movement, emphasize shapes, and bring whimsy to your patchwork. Be sure to consider using these designs for quilts that contain shapes that include 60° angles like hexagons and of course, equilateral triangles.

This chapter includes designs that create captivating textures and, depending on the intervals you choose, would be wonderful overall patterns that will enhance many larger quilts with ease.

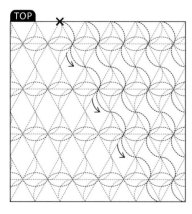

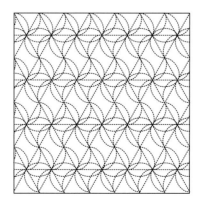

d

48

SASHIKO-INSPIRED DESIGNS

Sashiko is a traditional hand-embroidery technique that originated in Japan. Typically Sashiko is stitched by hand in white thread on indigo fabrics. It is the simple, geometric designs used in Sashiko that first caught my eye. Many Sashiko designs are grid based and composed of simple lines and gentle curves. Does that sound familiar? It certainly sounds walking-foot-friendly to me! To capitalize on the strengths of the walking foot, I took inspiration from traditional designs and adapted them to be continuous for machine quilting. I also borrowed the elements of Sashiko designs and created new designs that have a Sashiko-look and feel to me. These designs are perfect for quilts that call for simple yet interesting textures.

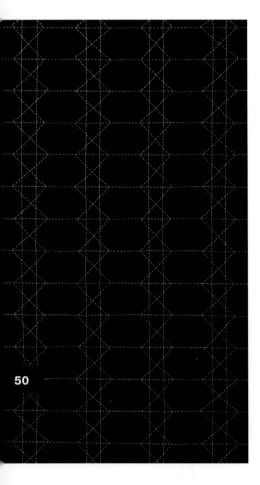

Diamond Ladder

Diamond Ladder is a moderately difficult design since it requires short point-to-point lines and a deep pivot. Use the knee lift or hover feature if available on your machine to make this design easier to quilt. Diamond Ladder provides an interesting texture and is a great overall design.

1. Using a fabric-safe marker, draw a line vertically from the top center to bottom center, parallel to the side of the quilt. Set the guide bar to a 2″ interval.

2. Align the guide bar with the marked line and echo quilt at the set interval to fill the right side of the quilt. (fig. a)

3. Rotate the quilt 180° and repeat Step 2 to complete the opposite side.

4. On the marked centerline from Step 1, mark another vertical line on the right, using your EFNI as the measurement. The quilt here has an EFNI of ½". Mark this line at the top so you can locate it again (fig. b). Quilt on the marked line. Quilt on the right side of the remainder of the vertical lines to fill in the right side of the quilt.

5. Rotate the quilt 180° and repeat Step 4 but this time quilt the line on the left of the previously quilted line. Quilt on the line.

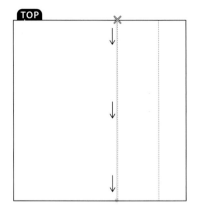

a

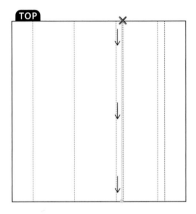

b

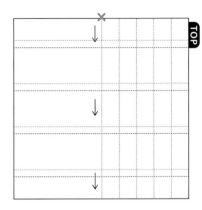

c

6. Rotate the quilt 90°. Draw a line vertically from the top center to bottom center parallel to the edge of one side of the quilt. Set the guide bar to a 1″ interval.

7. Align the guide bar with the marked line indicated here with the green line and Channel Quilt (see page 21), using a 1″ interval to fill in the right side of the quilt. (fig. c)

8. Rotate the quilt 180° and repeat Step 7 to fill in the opposite side of the quilt.

9. Rotate the quilt 90° and place a mark ¼″ on either side of the intersection of the pair of parallel lines (refer to the circle in Figure d for placement reference). (fig. d)

10. Starting at the top middle of the quilt, quilt point-to-point in a right to left zigzag pattern pivoting at each mark. Use the knee lift or hover feature to make pivoting easier for this design. Slide the quilt back through the harp and repeat the process in the opposite direction. (fig. e)

11. Repeat Step 10 to quilt the zigzag pattern on the remaining vertical lines on the right side of the quilt.

12. Rotate the quilt 180° and repeat Steps 10-11 to quilt the zigzag pattern on the vertical lines on the opposite side.

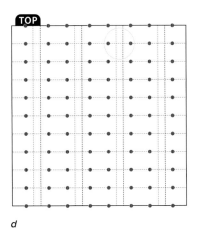

d

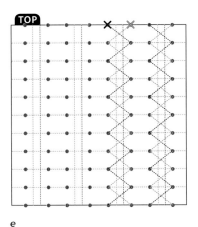

e

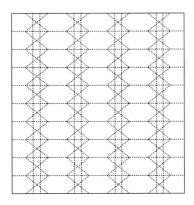

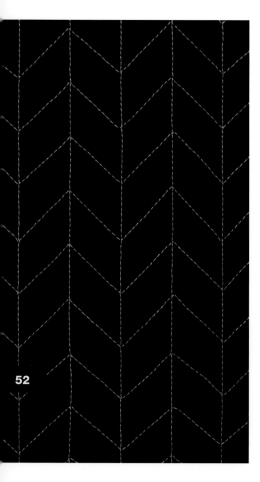

Sashiko Chevron

The Sashiko Chevron creates a beautifully simple texture with loads of movement by incorporating a Chevron pattern. It is fairly simple to quilt and quick to mark.

1. Starting at the top center, Channel Quilt (see page 21) across one side of the quilt top using a 1″ interval (**fig. a**). Rotate the quilt 180° and repeat to fill in the opposite side.

2. Rotate the quilt 90°. Use an acrylic ruler to mark two vertical rows of dots on each quilted line, 1″ apart. Quilt a point-to-point zigzag pattern pivoting at each dot. (**fig. b**)

3. Align the seam guide with the first zigzag line from Step 2 and tighten to set an accurate interval. Drop the needle one dot to the right of the red X and quilt the remainder of the zigzag lines. Repeat to fill in the top of the quilt. (**fig. c**)

4. Rotate the quilt 180° and repeat Step 3 to fill in the bottom half of the quilt to complete the design.

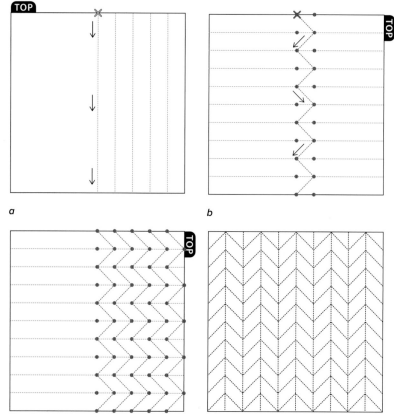

a

b

c

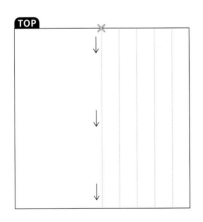

Arrows

Arrows is a simple textural design that combines Channel Quilting with point-to-point zigzag lines. I love the dimensional look. Arrows requires minimal marking if using a seam guide and is relatively quick to accomplish. Use the knee lift or hover feature if available on your machine to make pivoting easier.

1. Starting at the top center, Channel Quilt (see page 21) across one side of the quilt top using a 1″ interval. Rotate the quilt 180° and repeat to fill in the opposite side. **(fig. a)**

2. Rotate the quilt 90° and draw two perpendicular lines 1″ apart.

3. Starting at the red X, quilt point-to-point in a zigzag pattern, using the intersection of the quilted and drawn lines as pivot points. **(fig. b)**

4. Return to the top of the quilt and change the seam guide interval to 2″. Align it with the red X at the angle of the quilted line, noting that the seam guide will not be on the quilted line, but behind it. Quilt until you reach the first straight line and pivot, again aligning the seam guide with the next part of the zigzag line. This time the seam guide will be in front of the line. Continue this process to complete the next zigzag line and continue across the quilt to finish the right side.

5. Rotate the quilt 180° and repeat Step 4 to finish the design.

a

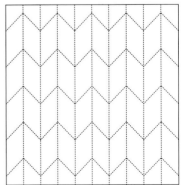

b

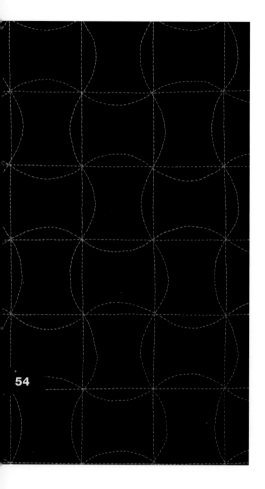

Apple Core

Apple Core combines a 90° grid with gentle curves to create a simple-to-quilt design with great movement and flow. The key to this design is the placement of the curves. Notice that within one square of the grid, two of the arcs curve into the square and the opposite two curve away from it.

1. Starting at the top center, Channel Quilt (see page 21) across one side of the quilt top using a 2″ interval. Rotate the quilt 180° and repeat to fill in the opposite side. Rotate the quilt 90° and repeat to create a grid.

2. Locate a vertical line approximately in the center of the quilt. Start at the red X and quilt gentle S-Curves from intersection to intersection. Make the depth of the curves about ¼″. Feel free to mark an additional dot at the deepest point of each curve or even mark the full curve if you prefer.

3. Quilt the next line with the same S-Curve pattern from Step 2 but start quilting in the opposite direction. Continue until the right side of the quilt is filled. (fig. a)

4. Rotate the quilt 180° and repeat the S-Curve pattern alternating the direction of the curve with each line. Quilt each line with S-Curves to finish the left side of the quilt. (fig. b)

5. Rotate the quilt 90° and repeat Steps 2-4 to complete the design, being sure the curves are placed correctly.

54

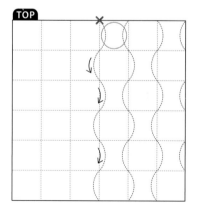

a

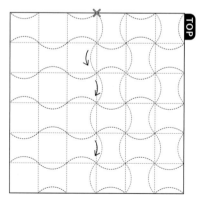

b

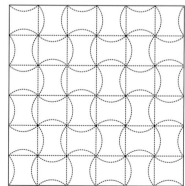

In and Out Curves

In and Out Curves is a variation of Apple Core since it is created by gentle curves and a 90° grid as well. Notice there are three arcs in one square of the grid while in the adjacent square, there is only one. My favorite part is how it almost looks like circles or bubbles and is just as simple to quilt.

1. Starting at the top center, Channel Quilt (see page 21) across one side of the quilt top using a 2″ interval. Rotate the quilt 180° and repeat to fill in the opposite side. Rotate the quilt 90° and repeat to create a grid.

2. Locate a vertical line in the approximate center of the quilt. Start at the red X and quilt gentle S-Curves from intersection to intersection. Make the depth of the curves about ¼″. Feel free to mark an additional dot at the deepest point of each curve or even mark the full curve if preferred. Making sure to start in the same direction, quilt each vertical line with the same S-Curve pattern to finish the right side of the quilt. (fig. a)

3. Rotate the quilt 180° and repeat Step 2 to finish the left side.

4. Rotate the quilt 90°. Starting at the green X, quilt S-Curves from intersection to intersection. Pay close attention to starting the curve in the correct direction as you quilt each line. Repeat to finish the right side. (fig. b)

5. Rotate the quilt 180° and repeat Step 4 to finish the left side and complete the design.

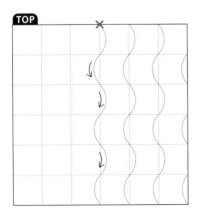

a

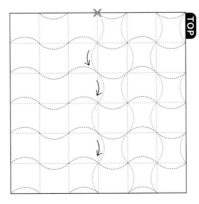

b

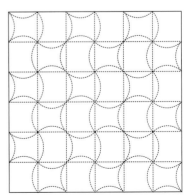

Sashiko Cubes

My favorite feature of the Sashiko Cubes design is its three dimensional quality. This design can transform a quilt into something special and it makes a wonderful whole-cloth design for a pillow. Sashiko Cubes is relatively simple to quilt especially on one that is pieced using identical squares, since they create a base-grid for the design; if not, the grid will need to be marked. Parts of the design also require frequent starting and stopping. Use the knee lift or hover feature if available to make pivoting easier in the point-to-point quilting of this design.

1. If there is not a grid to follow already formed by the piecing, mark a grid on the quilt top. My sample uses a 2″ marked grid.

2. Starting at the blue X, quilt point-to-point diagonally across two grid squares stopping at the marked intersection. Pivot and quilt diagonally across two marked grid squares in a zigzag pattern. **(fig. a)**

3. Return to the top of the quilt and repeat Step 2 starting at the red X and in the opposite direction to form diamonds. **(fig. b)**

4. Starting at the green X, one grid line to the right of the starting point in Step 2, quilt diagonally across a single grid

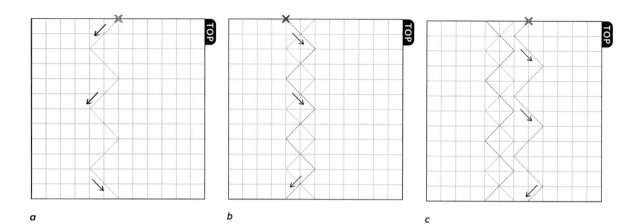

a

b

c

square. Pivot, then quilt diagonally across two grid squares and repeat in a zigzag pattern. **(fig. c)**

5. Return to the top of the quilt once again and, starting at the black X, repeat Step 4 in the opposite direction to form diamonds down the line. This row of diamonds will be offset from the first row. **(fig. d)**

6. Repeat Steps 2-5 to complete the right side of the quilt, then rotate the quilt 180° and repeat to fill in the left side.

7. Rotate the quilt 90° and begin by quilting the connecting lines that are 2 grid squares in length. Stop, skip two grid squares in length, then quilt the next two, etc. First, locate the bottom of a diamond near the top middle of the quilt. Drop the needle at the emerald X and secure using the tiny stitch method. Quilt along the marked grid line across two grid squares stopping at the intersection and secure again. Move the quilt through the harp to the bottom of the next diamond, skipping over two grid lines. Repeat this process down the vertical grid line and for the remainder of the grid lines on the right side of the quilt.

8. Rotate the quilt 180° and complete the connecting lines on the opposite side to complete the design. **(fig. e)**

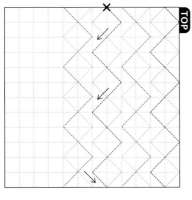

d

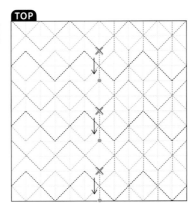

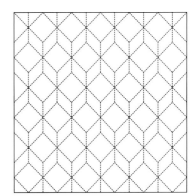

e

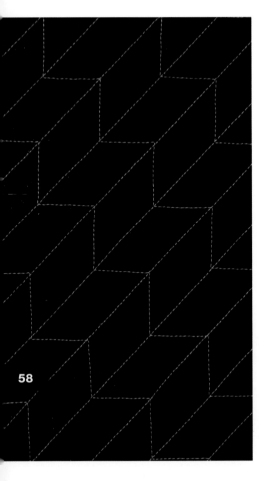

Dimensional Arrows

Like Sashiko Cubes, Dimensional Arrows also has that special three-dimensional quality. The 90° pivot is challenging, so use the knee lift or hover feature if available to keep your hands free to move the quilt and make the pivot.

1. Using your acrylic ruler, place the 45° line along the bottom edge of the quilt top so that there is approximately half of the quilt top on either side. Make sure the ruler is angled to the right at 45° (fig. a). Draw a line across the quilt.

2. Set the seam guide interval to 1″, align the seam guide with the drawn line and Channel Quilt (see page 21) to fill the area.

3. Starting in the left upper corner, mark 90° stair-stepped lines from the upper left to the bottom right. Quilt the pattern from point-to-point, pivoting at the quilted intersections. (fig. b)

4. Skip one diagonal line and drop the needle at the top of the next diagonal line. Align the seam guide with the previously quilted line from Step 3 and set that interval. Quilt the stair step pattern using the seam guide and quilted diagonal lines as turning points to fill in the right side.

5. Rotate the quilt 180° and repeat Step 4 to finish the opposite side. It may be tricky to find the starting point after rotating. To help, draw the initial stair step pattern for the opposite side. Once you have found the pattern, start at the top and use the guide bar to quilt as in Step 4.

a

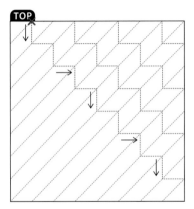

b

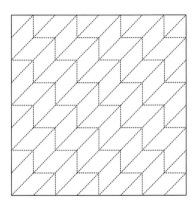

58

Sashiko Diamonds

Sashiko diamonds is based on a 90° grid with point-to-point diamonds intersecting in the grid squares. It looks complex but is really straightforward and creates a lovely motif.

1. Starting at the top center, Channel Quilt (see page 21) across one side of the quilt top using a 1″ interval. Rotate the quilt 180° and repeat to fill in the opposite side. Rotate the quilt a further 90° and repeat to create a grid.

2. Using a fabric-safe marker, mark dots ¼″ away from both sides of every other grid intersection. **(fig. a)**

3. Quilt from the red X across first square, then point-to-point in a zigzag pattern across two grid square lengths using the dots and intersections as guides for pivoting. Slide the quilt back through the harp and repeat the process to form the diamonds. Continue this to finish the right side of the quilt.

4. Rotate the quilt 180° and repeat Step 3 to finish the left side.

5. Rotate the quilt 90° and repeat Steps 2-4 making sure that the rows of diamonds are positioned correctly on every other line. **(fig. b)**

6. Repeat Step 4 again to quilt point-to-point diamonds across the quilt to finish the design.

59

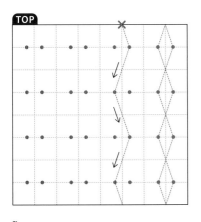

a

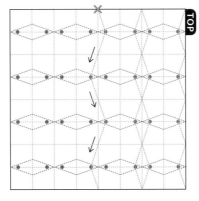

b

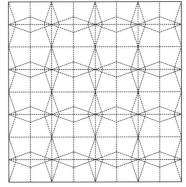

Windsails

Windsails uses a combination of gentle arcs and a foundational grid to create a design with surprising dimensionality and an abundance of movement.

1. Starting at the top center, Channel Quilt (see page 21) across the entire quilt top using a 2½″ interval. Rotate the quilt 180° and Channel Quilt to fill in the opposite side. Rotate the quilt 90° and repeat to create a grid.

2. Start on the center vertical line and quilt shallow arcs from intersection to intersection. Repeat this process on the vertical lines to finish the left side. Rotate the quilt 180° and repeat to finish the right side. **(fig. a)**

3. Rotate the quilt 90° and repeat Step 2. **(fig. b)**

4. Position the quilt so that the arcs form an L-shape. Start on the largest diagonal and quilt arcs from intersection to intersection pivoting on the grid lines **(fig. c)**. Rotate the quilt 180° and quilt the remaining diagonal arcs to complete the design.

60

TIP: Because the curves are so shallow, it is reasonably simple to quilt without marking, though you are welcome to. The most difficult curve to quilt without marking is the diagonal because there is no reference line. If marking, invest time in the diagonal curve. My quilted sample uses a 2½″ grid, the edge of a 4″ diameter circle to mark the horizontal and vertical arcs, and a 8″ diameter circle to mark the diagonal arcs.

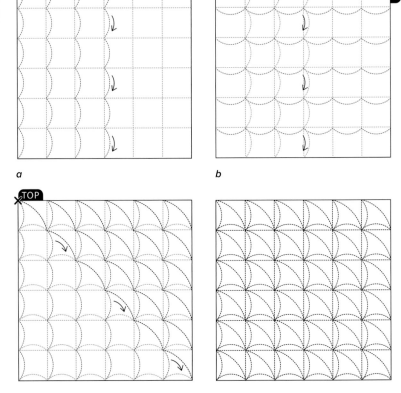

a

b

c

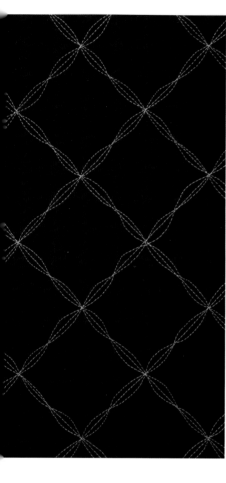

Trellis

Trellis is a light, floral whimsical design set on an on-point 90° grid. Larger interval grids work better with Trellis as they provide more room for quilting the S-Curves within each grid line. My quilted sample uses a 2½″ interval.

1. Draw a diagonal line to divide the quilt in half. Draw a second diagonal line intersecting the first at 90°.

2. Set the seam guide to the desired interval. Align it with the left-leaning diagonal line from Step 1. Quilt lines to fill the right side. Rotate the quilt 180° and repeat to fill in the left side.

3. Rotate the quilt 90°. Repeat Steps 2-3 to finish the grid.

4. Mark the center of each grid line on the left-leaning diagonal lines and quilt a gentle S-Curve on alternating sides of the line, pivoting at each mark and grid intersection. **(fig. a)**

5. Repeat Step 4 on the opposite sides of the line. **(fig. b)**

6. Rotate the quilt 90° and repeat Steps 4-5. **(figs. c & d)**

61

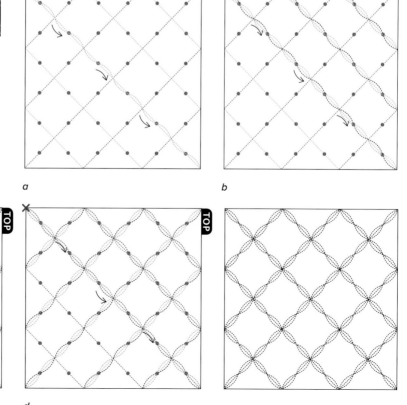

a

b

c

d

Ribbon Pinwheels

The Ribbon Pinwheels design is full of movement and flow and is a simple design to mark and quilt. The grid size can easily be made larger or smaller while maintaining the integrity of the design, and the depth of the curves can be adjusted to change the difficulty level and density. Like the Trellis design, Ribbon Pinwheels has enough complexity to make it interesting, but not too much so as to result in overly-dense quilting. It is a lovely design for any quilt that cries out for a lot of movement and a little bit of fun.

1. Starting at the top center, Channel Quilt (see page 21) across the entire quilt top using a 2½″ interval. Rotate the quilt 180° and Channel Quilt to fill in the opposite side. Rotate the quilt 90° and repeat to create a grid.

2. Starting at the middle top vertical line, mark crescent moon shapes as shown in Figure a.

3. Quilt the moon shapes in two parts. For the first part, start at the middle top vertical line, indicated here with the red X, and quilt an S-Curve down the line starting on the outer curve and pivoting slightly at each grid intersection. **(fig. a)**

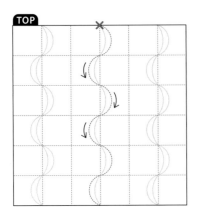

a

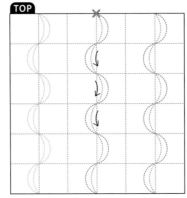

b

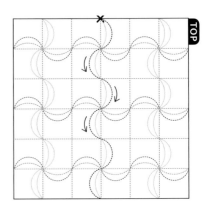

c

4. Slide the quilt back through the harp and start the second part on the inner curve, moving to the next inner curve in a similar S-Curve motion all the way down the quilt. (fig. b)

5. Repeat Steps 3-4 for every other vertical line to complete the right side of the quilt.

6. Rotate the quilt 180° and repeat Steps 3-4 to complete the left side of the quilt.

7. Rotate the quilt 90° and repeat Steps 2-6 starting first on the outer curve, indicated here with a black line, and then coming back up and echoing with a shalllower curve, indicated here in emerald. Make sure that the crescent moon shapes are marked on every other line so that they form the desired pinwheel design. (figs. c & d)

- -

TIP: Consider making a crescent moon-shaped template to ease the marking of the Ribbon Pinwheels design. To do this, cut a cardboard square the size of your grid interval: I used a 2½˝ square. Draw a horizontal line across the square to divide it in half. Mark dots ½˝ and 1˝ inside the left edge along the marked horizontal line. Use circle templates or a small curved cup or plate to trace arcs from the top to bottom corners through the dots. I used a 4˝ circle and the top of my spray baste can which is a 2½˝ circle. Cut out the moon shape to use as a template for tracing your Ribbon Pinwheels.

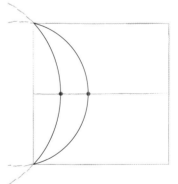

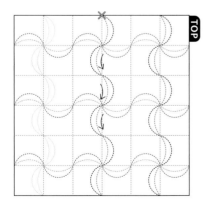

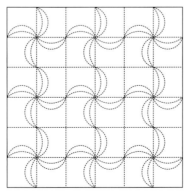

d

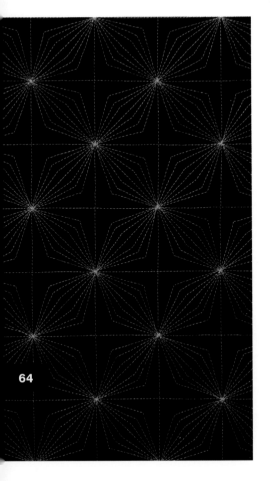

Hemp Leaf Variation

The Hemp Leaf Variation is a nod to the traditional Sashiko Hemp Leaf pattern. This design has only four leaves instead of the traditional six, but the added intricacy compensates for the missing leaves. Hemp Leaf is a versatile design because it can easily be adapted by changing the size of the grid and adding or subtracting lines from the radiating diamonds in each grid square.

1. Starting at the top center, Channel Quilt (see page 21) across the entire quilt top using a 2″ interval. Rotate the quilt 180° and Channel Quilt to fill in the opposite side. Rotate the quilt 90° and repeat to create a grid.

2. Draw a diagonal line from intersection to intersection at the widest point of the quilt to divide it into two parts. Quilt along the marked line. Quilt along every other diagonal line through the intersections of the grid squares to fill in the right side of the quilt. **(fig. a)**

3. Rotate the quilt 180° and repeat Step 2 to fill in the left side. Make sure to quilt alternating diagonal lines.

4. Rotate the quilt 90° and repeat Steps 2-3 to complete the diagonal grid, indicated here in green. Again make sure

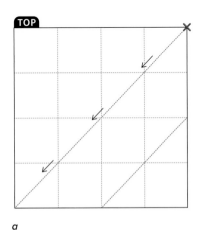

a

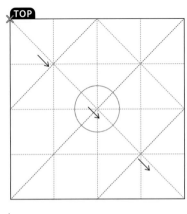

b

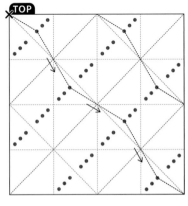

c

you only quilt every other diagonal line. Also ensure that the second set of diagonal lines intersects the first set of diagonal lines at the corners of the grid squares. **(fig. b)**

5. On both sides of the quilted lines from Step 4, mark ¼″, ½″ and ¾″ away from either side of the line, so that there are six markings within each grid square. See the Tip on the right. Repeat this set of markings for every grid square within every other diagonal row.

6. Quilt point-to-point in a zigzag pattern on either side of the line from Step 4. Work from grid intersection to inner dot, to the next intersection, then to the next inner dot. **(fig. c)**

7. Slide the quilt back through the harp and quilt the opposite side in the same way to form a skinny diamond.

8. Repeat Steps 6-7 for the middle and outer marked dots. Continue quilting the remainder of the diagonals in this manner to complete the right side of the quilt. **(fig. d)**

9. Rotate the quilt 180° and repeat Steps 6-8 to complete the left side of the quilt.

10. Rotate the quilt 90° and repeat Steps 5-9 for the right-leaning diagonals to complete the design. **(fig. e)**

TIP: Consider making a simple marking template to speed up the marking process for this design. To do this, cut a 3″ × 1″ cardboard rectangle and draw a line to mark the center. In a different colored ink, draw lines ¼″, ½″, ¾″ away from the center line on both sides. You can use this to easily mark the remaining quilt top.

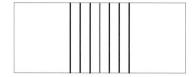

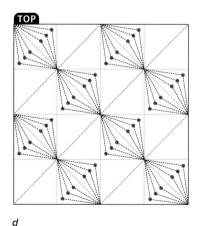

d

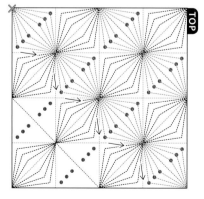

e

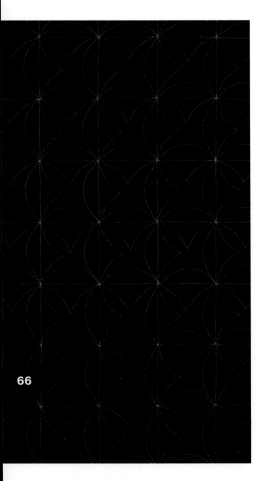

Wings

Everyone needs a challenge, right? Well, Wings is the most challenging design in this chapter. While it sits on a simple grid, the curves in this design are deep and require a high-level of quilt manipulation skills...especially for a large quilt. The larger the grid, the less difficult the quilting will be. The knee lift or hover feature will also support hands free pivoting which will make manipulating the quilt easier. My quilted sample uses a 2½˝ interval grid.

1. Starting at the top center, Channel Quilt (see page 21) across the entire quilt top using a 2½˝ interval. Rotate the quilt 180° and Channel Quilt to fill in the opposite side. Rotate the quilt 90° and repeat to create a grid.

2. Using a fabric-safe marker, mark the clamshell design on each vertical grid line. Start at the center vertical and quilt the long arcs from intersection to intersection down the line. Repeat on all the vertical lines to complete the right side of the quilt. (fig. c)

TIP: Marking the Wings design is easiest when using a clamshell template. Cut a cardboard square the size of the grid square. My square is 2½˝. Draw a line 2˝ away from the left edge of the square. Mark the center point of this line. Then, mark a dot ¾˝ inside the left edge at both the top and bottom of the square. Connect the dots with arcs as shown in Figure a. Use the edge of a small circle to mark the arcs. Figure b shows how a template can be adapted if you are quilting shallower arcs.

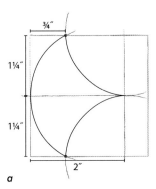

a

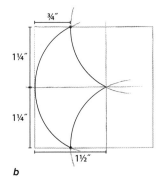

b

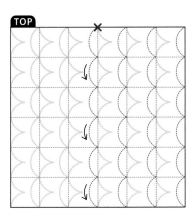

c

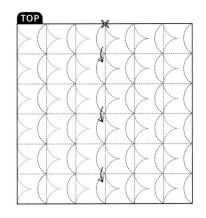

d

3. Return to the center vertical and quilt the double arcs from intersection to intersection, indicated here in green. Repeat on all the vertical lines to complete the right side of the quilt. **(fig. d)**

4. Rotate the quilt 180° and repeat Steps 3-4 to complete the left side of the quilt.

5. Rotate the quilt 90° and repeat Steps 2-4 to complete the design **(figs. e & f)**. Double-check to make sure that the clamshells are marked correctly as in the red circle in Figure g.

- -

TIP: While the original design is a challenging one, Figure b can easily be altered to make it more accessible for a beginner quilter by reducing the pivot required on the double arc side of the design (shown in the red circle in Figure g).

SEND OFF

A few years ago I made a special quilt inspired by one of my quilting heroes, Yoshiko Jinzenji. I used fabric designed by her that called for quilting that provided a feeling of cleanliness and simplicity. I used a Sashiko-inspired point-to-point design from my first *WALK* book. It was that quilt and that design that set me on the path to creating additional Sashiko-inspired designs. The designs in this chapter are primarily grid based and can add structure and repetition to a quilt design. In addition to the structural component, the designs have intricacy, movement and charm. They command attention yet are subtle enough not to overwhelm.

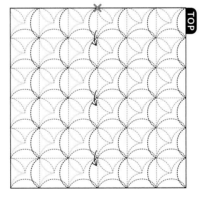

e   f

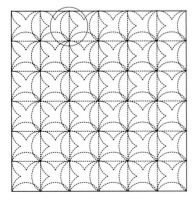

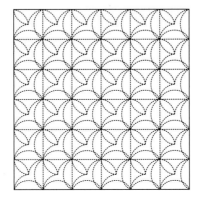

g

"Rotational designs add a unique flair to your quilts and have the potential to highlight your piecing and elevate your quilts.

ROTATIONAL DESIGNS

YOU SPIN ME RIGHT ROUND

Rotational designs are a new design category for me and I'm so excited to share them with you. Anita Shackleford introduced me to rotational quilting when she shared her Perfect Spiral tool (see page 175) with me at Quilter's Affair in Sisters, Oregon. I've used Anita's tool and her rotational lines and arcs on many quilts. When working on my Quiet Geometry quilt (see page 140) I needed interesting designs for the circles, so I began experimenting with the idea of rotating shapes instead of arcs. I found that if I kept the shapes walking-foot-friendly by using only simple lines and gentle curves, these rotational designs had potential. In fact, they have now become a staple in my quilting toolbox.

Essentially, rotational quilting involves choosing a shape or a line, aligning the focal point to the center of a circle and then rotating the shape or line around the circle at equal intervals. Rotational designs require extensive marking and turning, but they are well worth that investment of time. Start practicing on small projects and as you become more proficient you might be surprised at how large a quilt you are willing to tackle with rotational designs. Since the marking and quilting technique is similar for all the designs in this chapter, I'm sharing the information that will be applicable to all of the designs first and then each specific one will be highlighted later in the chapter.

Tools and Techniques

Rotational quilting requires a few simple tools. The first tool you'll need is a compass. I purchased a carpenter's compass (pictured below, see page 175) since it is inexpensive and allows me to draw very large circles with ease.

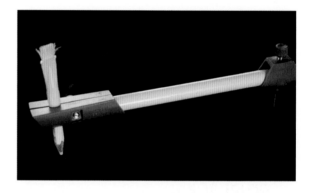

If you don't want to purchase a commercial one, make a simple string compass instead.

Making and Using a String Compass

MATERIALS

→ String

→ Fabric-safe marking pencil

→ Pin

1. Wrap and tie a piece of string low down around the marking pencil. Place a mark on the string the length of the radius away from the pencil.

GEOMETRY NOTE: Remember that the radius is the line from the center to the edge of a circle.

2. Hold or pin the mark on the string at the center-point of the circle. Draw the circle with the pencil keeping the string taut and the pencil upright.

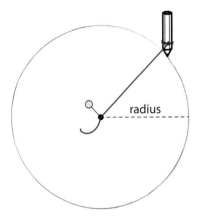

Interval Marking Tool

The other tool I use for rotational quilting is an interval marker. I have designed three versions of this tool for dividing and marking circles into equal intervals (pictured on the right). Tool A divides the circle into 6, 12 or 24 equal intervals. Tool B divides the circle into 8, 16 or 32 equal intervals. Tool C divides the circle into 9, 18 or 36 equal intervals. Use the outer ring to mark the large intervals (6, 8, or 9 sections), the second ring to mark the medium intervals (12, 16 or 18 sections) and the inner ring to mark the smallest intervals (24, 32, or 36 sections).

Full size versions of the interval marking tools are found on page 174.

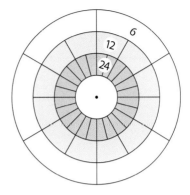

Interval Marking Tool A

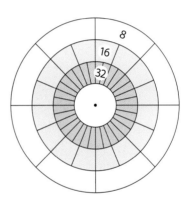

Interval Marking Tool B

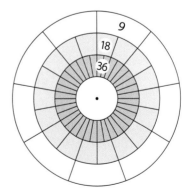

Interval Marking Tool C

Marking the Intervals

1. On the quilt top, mark the center-point of the design with a dot. The diameter of the circle will determine the size of the quilted design.

GEOMETRY NOTE: The diameter is a line from edge to edge of a circle through the center. The diameter measures twice the radius of the circle.

2. Set the compass to the radius of the desired circle size. Place its point onto the marked dot from Step 1 and draw the circle.

3. Decide on the number of rotations desired. To help make this decision, I usually draw the design on paper to see how different numbers of rotations look. This also allows me to make any adjustments to the line or shape to get the look I desire before committing to the quilt.

4. Choose the interval tool that works to mark your chosen number of rotations. Put a pin through the center of the tool and align with the marked center-point from Step 1. Tape or use of few dots of glue to secure the interval tool to the fabric so it doesn't move as you mark.

5. Align a ruler with the selected line in the ring of the tool and the center-point of the shape. Using a fabric-safe, marker, mark the interval on the outer ring of the drawn circle. Working clockwise, rotate the ruler keeping one edge at the center-point and with the next line in the ring. Continue marking around the outside of the circle as you rotate the ruler. Remove the interval tool and the circle

will be divided into even intervals, ready to mark with a template.

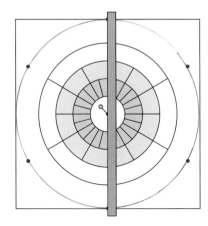

MARKING INTERVALS IN A BLOCK

1. On the quilt top, mark the center-point of the block with a dot.

2. Put a pin through the center of the interval tool and the marked center-point from Step 1. Tape or use a of few dots of glue to secure the interval tool to the fabric so it doesn't move as you mark.

3. Align a ruler with the selected line in the ring of the tool and the center-point of the shape. Using a fabric-safe, marker, mark the interval on the outer edge of the block.

4. Rotate the ruler clockwise, positioning it on each line in the ring and the marked center-point from Step 1. Continue marking around the perimeter of the block. Remove the interval tool and the block will be marked with even intervals and ready to mark with a linear or shape template.

Choosing a Shape or Line

Deciding what to rotate is the fun part. The same line or shape creates a different design depending on the placement of the rotational focal point and the number of rotations.

I always test an idea on paper before I commit to making it part of a quilting plan. Here, I experimented with two different focal points of an elongated pentagon (fig a). The pentagon is rotated the same number of times, but even though the shape is the same, the difference in the focal point significantly changes the look of the design. (figs. b & c)

In addition to varying the position of the focal point, the number of rotations impacts the look of the design. The more frequently the shape is rotated, the denser the quilting becomes and it becomes more difficult to execute. (figs. d & e)

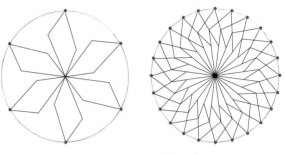

d: 6 rotations   e: 24 rotations

When many lines overlap, especially near the center (fig. e), the quilting becomes challenging. While close spacing shouldn't necessarily be avoided, a slight alteration in shape makes a big difference in reducing the density without a big impact on the overall look. Widening a shape slightly, for example (figs. f & g), reduces the overlap in the center, making it easier to quilt. As designs get larger, they also become easier to quilt, since the lines will be farther apart. As you finalize your designs, consider adjusting a favorite shape just slightly as below.

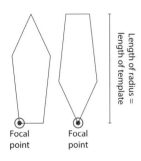

Length of radius = length of template

Focal point   Focal point

a

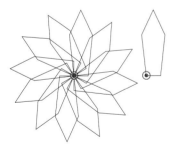

b

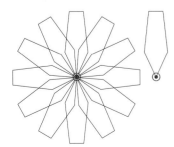

c

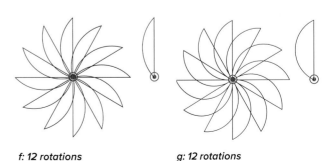

f: 12 rotations   g: 12 rotations

Making Design Templates

Each design in this chapter requires a template to mark the design. Making them is simple and they can be customized for each project. The length of the template can vary and can range from typical block sizes to supersized templates for quilting one rotational design to fill an entire quilt. For anything larger than 12″ blocks, I tape comic book boards together to make the template. Comic book boards are readily available, easy to cut and are thicker than cardstock so they can stand up to repeated tracing. Feel free to enlarge the shapes in the book, but don't be afraid to draw and cut your own.

TIP: Since comic book boards are stiff and not easy to fold, draw and cut the shape on paper and then trace the completed template onto the comic book board and cut out.

MAKING LINEAR TEMPLATES

1. Determine the design and placement on the quilt. If the design will be within a circle, measure the radius **(fig. a)**. If the design will be within a block, measure from the center point to a corner **(fig. b)**. This will be the length of the template.

5. Cut along the drawn line to create the template. Use the left side as the template and the flipped version will be the mirror image template. **(fig. e)**

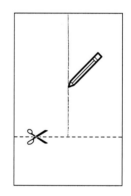

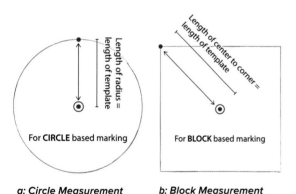

a: Circle Measurement   b: Block Measurement

For **CIRCLE** based marking — Length of radius = length of template

For **BLOCK** based marking — Length of center to corner = length of template

c

2. Cut the board to the measurement from Step 1.

3. Draw a vertical line down the center of the board. **(fig. c)**

4. Draw the linear design so that the top and bottom of the design align with the top and bottom of the vertical line drawn in Step 3. **(fig. d)**

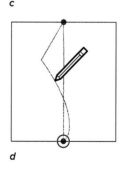

d

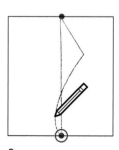

e

MAKING SHAPE TEMPLATES

Making templates for the shape-based rotational designs means cutting out shapes that are the correct length for the design area you are using. As with the linear templates, the length of the template from focal point to tip should equal the radius of the circle that will contain the design or, if using in a block, the distance from the center of the block to a corner.

Symmetrical shapes

To make symmetrical shape templates like the Elongated Diamond (see page 91), use the three steps listed below. Use the template illustration for each symmetrical shape in the chapter as your guide.

1. Cut the board or paper to the correct length.

2. Fold in half lengthwise and draw half of the shape on one side of the folded edge and cut along those drawn lines. **(fig. f)**

3. Unfold to reveal the template.

f

Asymmetrical shapes

To make asymmetrical templates like the Obtuse Triangle (see page 88), draw the entire shape and cut it out. Use the template illustration for each asymmetrical shape in the chapter as your guide. Don't worry if the shape isn't duplicated exactly. In fact, you may create a new version with your own hand drawing. All of these are simple shapes even though they look complex. Find a favorite and dive in. You can do it!

1. Determine the length of the template (see above). Use the template cutting diagram for the shape to determine whether to cut the paper larger than the length of the template as in Figure g since the point of the triangle extends beyond the template length.

2. Draw the shape.

3. Cut on the lines to create the template.

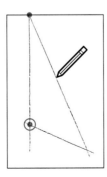

g

Marking the Designs

With the quilting area identified, the intervals marked, the template made and the focal point chosen, you are ready to mark the design itself. Marking pencils that make a fine line work best for marking these designs.

MARKING WITHIN A CIRCLE

1. Place the template with the focal point on the center of the circle and the tip of the shape on one of the interval marks.

2. Trace around the template with a fabric-safe marker. (fig. a)

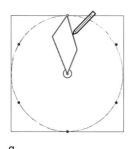 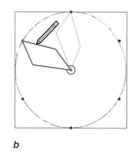

a   b

3. Move the template, aligning the tip with the next interval mark and keeping the focal point on the center of the circle. Continue to rotate the template from mark to mark, tracing around it each time until there is a shape at each interval. (fig. b)

TIP: **If you are nervous about marking a design with lots of rotations, mark and quilt half of a design at a time. For example, mark a 12-interval rotation, quilt along those markings and then come back and mark an additional 12 intervals for a total of 24. Designs with many lines can definitely get confusing and it is easy to lose your place, especially if it is your first time quilting rotational designs.**

MARKING WITHIN A BLOCK

1. Ensure the template length is based on the measurement of the center point to a corner. Mark only to the edge of the block even if the template extends past the perimeter in places. Using a pushpin or Hera marker, lightly score down the centerline on both sides of the template. Fold on the scored line.

TIP: **If the template is not symmetrical, score from the tip to the focal point along that imaginary line as shown in each cutting diagram.**

2. Unfold the template and position it so the focal point is on the center of the block and the tip is in a corner. Trace around the template. (fig. c)

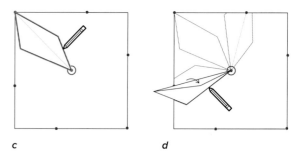

c   d

3. Move the template to the next interval mark, keeping the focal point on the center. **Align the fold** with the interval mark. Unfold and trace around the template. Continue this process until there is a shape at each interval. (fig. d)

VARIATIONS

If the edge of the shape template is a straight line as for the curved slice shape, align the straight line with the interval markings (fig. e). Linear templates work the same way. Align the straight edge of the template with the interval marking and then trace the line or arc. (fig. f)

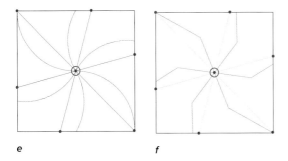

e   f

Quilting the Designs

The great thing about rotational designs is that many can be quilted continuously, but typically there is lots of turning required. Linear and shape-based rotations differ a bit in the quilting process, but all use the 'following a marked line' technique (see page 19). The first two lines or shapes you quilt will establish the center intersection. If the markings at the center of the circle don't align after you have quilted a few lines, trust yourself, not the markings and make adjustments if needed. Use the 'where-you-look-is-where-you-quilt' technique to hit the center point that is established where your first two lines intersect. It is the quilted lines that will show in the end.

QUILTING LINEAR ROTATIONAL DESIGNS

As I mentioned earlier, this journey began using simple rotational arcs. Lines and gentle curves can be combined to create intriguing yet simple-to-quilt rotational designs. Linear designs will typically not be continuous unless they are alternated with regular and mirror image marking (see page 102). The number of rotations, the complexity of the shape, and the size of the quilt will determine the difficulty level of the quilting. The key to linear rotations is to get the lines to meet cleanly at the center point. If you're quilting a single linear rotation, the design won't be continuous.

Quilting Edge to Edge

To quilt a single linear design (figs. g & h), quilt edge to-edge through the center, securing the thread at both ends of the line with the tiny stitch method (see page 87). If you begin and end off the quilt top and move out onto the batting, there is no need to secure your stitches. Repeat this process for each line in the rotation until the design is complete.

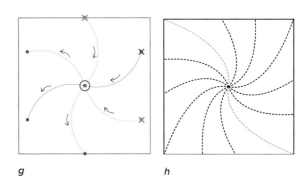

g   h

LINEAR DESIGN OPTIONS

In this section, I share seven linear rotational designs. Linear rotations are not limited to only these options, so feel free to experiment with your own ideas once you get the hang of the basics. The designs begin with the simplest and move to a final design called Five, that I created for the set of quilts I made celebrating the fifth anniversary of the MQG's annual quilt show, QuiltCon. I included Five because I want to spark your creativity and open your mind to the possibility of designing your own unique linear rotation. For each design, I indicate the focal point, illustrate how to draw and cut the template, show you how the design looks with additional rotations added, and share a quilted example I made for you. All of my samples are quilted using 24 rotations. Remember that detailed instructions for marking the intervals, making the templates, marking the designs and quilting the designs are on pages 71-77. Each of these linear designs may be quilted within a circle or a block.

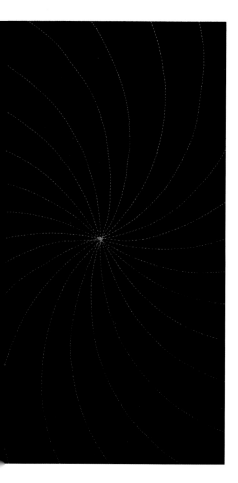

Arc

Design Sample Size   18″ in diameter

Template Length   9″

Marking Tool   Use the edge of a 12″ diameter circle to mark the arc. I used my 12″ nested circle template. (Resources page 175) or cut an arc template using the cutting diagram.

Tips   Arcs is an asymmetrical design, so mirror image marking will be necessary for block-based continuous quilting.

Adjusting the Difficulty   Mark gentler arcs with a larger diameter circle to reduce the difficulty. A curved arc with a smaller radius will be more challenging to quilt since it requires more turning of the quilt.

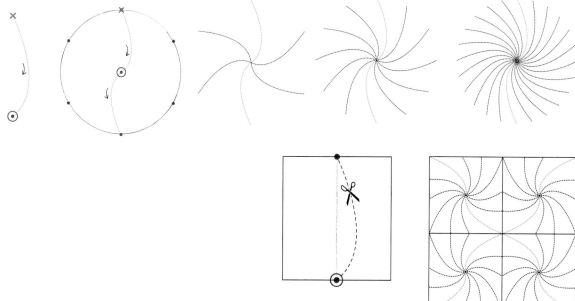

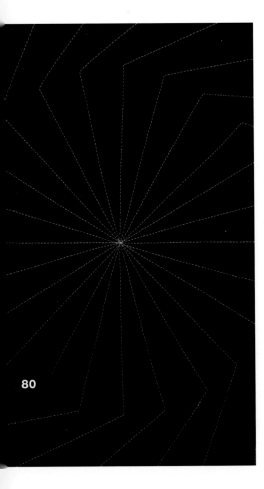

Bent Line

Design Sample Size   18″ in diameter

Template Length   9″

Marking Tool   Ruler

Tips   Use the knee lift or hover tool to make pivoting from line to line easier. Bent Line is an asymmetrical design so mirror image marking will be necessary for block based continuous quilting.

Adjusting the Difficulty   Lessen the angle of the pivot in the bent line to make the quilt easier to turn. Increasing the pivot angle will result in a more challenging design.

Design Variations   Different pivot angles in the bent line can significantly change the look of this design. The lengths of the two lines can also be varied. Making one very short and one long, will result in a big change in the appearance of the design.

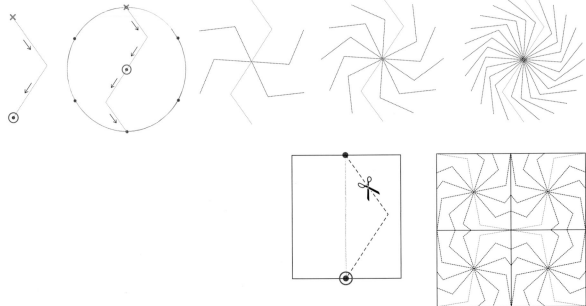

Lightning Bolt

Design Sample Size   18″ in diameter

Template Length   9″

Marking Tool   Ruler

Tips   Use the knee lift or hover tool to make pivoting from line to line easier. Lightning Bolt is an asymmetrical design so mirror image marking will be necessary for block based continuous quilting.

Adjusting the Difficulty   Variations in the angle of the two pivots affect the difficulty of this design. Shallow pivots are easier to quilt, while deep ones require more movement of the quilt so are more difficult.

Design Variations   Lightning Bolt is essentially a variation of the Bent Line design. Instead of the three lines I've used, could you do more? Play around with this one!

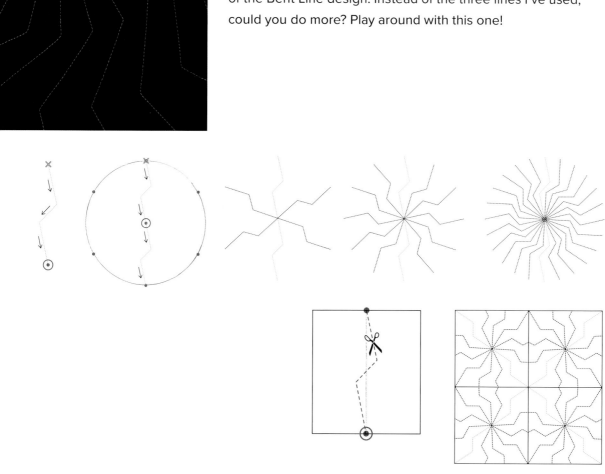

Arc/Line Combo 1

Design Sample Size 18″ in diameter

Template Length 9″

Marking Tool Use the edge of a 6″ diameter circle template to mark the arc and a ruler to mark the line.

Tips Use the knee lift or hover tool on your machine to make pivoting easier. Arc/Line Combo 1 is an asymmetrical design, so mirror image marking will be necessary for block based continuous quilting.

Adjusting the Difficulty Mark the arc with a larger diameter circle to lessen both the curve and reduce the pivoting between the line and the arc. This reduces the amount of turning. You can also increase the difficulty by deepening the pivot between the line and the arc.

Design Variations Changing the angle of the pivot between the line and the arc and the depth of the arc will also affect the look. Try one line and two arcs, or try different combinations of lines and arcs or different line lengths for other looks.

82

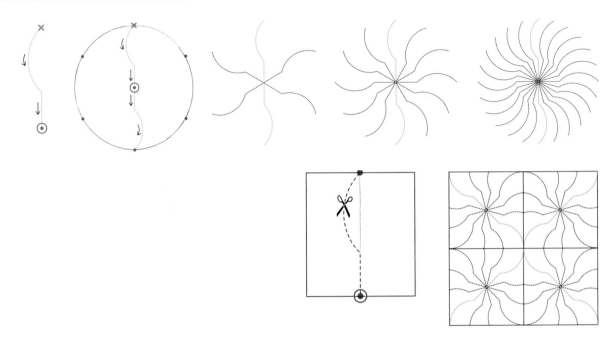

Arc/Line Combo 2

Design Sample Size   18˝ in diameter

Template Length   9˝

Marking Tool   Use the edge of a 6˝ diameter circle template to mark the arc and a ruler to mark the line.

Tips   This design uses the same template as Arc/Line Combo 1, but changes the focal point to the end of the arc rather than the end of the line. Use the knee lift or hover tool on your machine to make pivoting from line to line easier. Arc/Line Combo 2 is an asymmetrical design so mirror image marking will be necessary for block-based continuous quilting.

Adjusting the Difficulty   Mark the arc with a larger diameter circle to lessen the curve of the arc thereby reducing the pivoting between the line and the arc. This reduces the amount of turning. You can also increase the difficulty by deepening the pivot between the line and the arc.

Design Variations   Changing the pivot angle between the line and the arc and the depth of the arc will affect the look. Try one line and two arcs or different line lengths for another look.

83

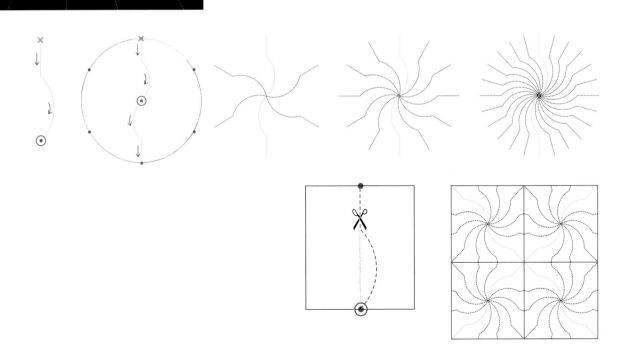

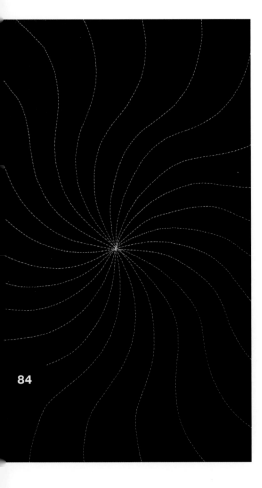

S-Curve

Design Sample Size 18″ in diameter

Template Length 9″

Marking Tool Use the edge of an 8″ diameter circle template to mark the two arcs of the S-Curve.

Tips S-Curves is an asymmetrical design, so mirror image marking will be necessary for block-based continuous quilting.

Adjusting the Difficulty Keep the arcs large and shallow to lessen the difficulty. Combining a large sweeping arc with a small deeper arc will be more challenging to quilt.

Design Variations Any S-Curve can be used for this design. The arcs could be identical or they could be different depths. Could you even do a triple S-Curve?

84

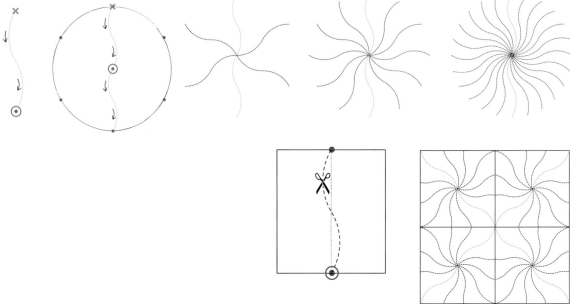

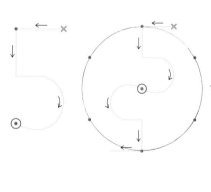

Five

Design Sample Size   18″ in diameter

Template Length   9″

Marking Tool   I used the edge of a 5″ circle template for the curved part of the Five and a ruler for the lines.

Tips   I cut the board for the template 8½″ × 11″ and drew the vertical line 2″ away from the left edge. I drew the number '5' 1″ from the top and bottom of the template to create a 9″ template. When marking, align the tip of the bottom curve with the center point in the circle and the inside corner (marked with a red dot in the illustration) of the top of the '5' with an interval mark. I also recommend rotating the template no more than 12 times. Too many rotations will obscure the visibility of the design. Note: Five does not work for continuous quilting.

Adjusting the Difficulty   Because of the deep curve, this is a challenging design, requiring lots of movement of the quilt. I recommend using Five for only small projects.

Design Variations   I wanted to share this variation of a linear design so that you will be inspired to use this method to customize a design of your own for a special project.

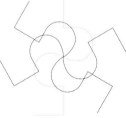
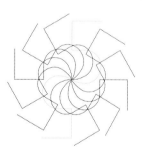
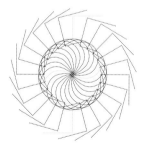

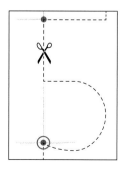
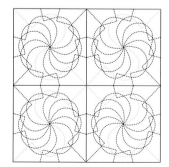

SHAPE-BASED DESIGN OPTIONS

The options are limitless for shape-based rotational designs. As with the linear designs, I've organized these by their shape and from the easiest to more challenging within each shape. For each design, I indicate the focal point, illustrate the drawing and cutting of the template, illustrate different rotations and share a quilted example. The quilted samples all have 24 rotations. I've also included information that will help you quilt each design successfully if they are quilted continuously in blocks. Detailed instructions for marking the intervals, making the templates and marking the designs are on pages 71-77. Each of these shape-based designs may be quilted within a circle or confined to a block.

Quilting Shape-Based Rotations

Shape-based rotational designs are quilted continuously with lots of turning. The number of rotations, the complexity of the shape, the size of the design, the size of the quilt itself and your level of experience will all combine to determine the difficulty. It is important to take all of these factors into consideration before tackling a quilt.

1. This is my tiny stitch method: Start quilting in the center of the marked design. Align the needle with the center point and pull up the bobbin thread. Set your stitch length to .2 and secure by quilting 5 to 7 tiny stitches.

2. Return the stitch length to the normal quilting length and quilt on the drawn lines, pivoting with the needle down at any turn points. Quilt the first shape and return to the center point. With the needle down, lift the presser foot to adjust it and turn the quilt to aim for the next shape. Quilt the next marked shape, again returning to the center. **(fig. a)**

3. Repeat this process for each marked shape in the design.

4. When all the shapes have been quilted and you've returned to the center of the design, drop the stitch length to .2 again. Stitch 5 to 7 stitches to secure and clip the threads to finish.

TIP: The quilting order of the shapes is up to you but it should depend upon where the design is marked and which turning direction works better for you to manage the bulk of the quilt. You may quilt shape-by-shape around the circle or shapes directly across from each other and then quilt the next pair of shapes continuing around the circle. I tend to progress in order around the circle so I don't get lost in the lines.

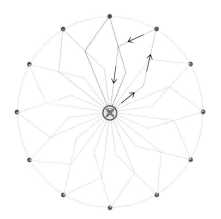

Figure a

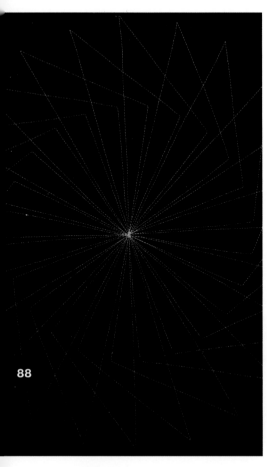

Obtuse Triangle

Sample Design Size   18″ in diameter

Template Length   9″

Marking Tool   Ruler

Tips   The key to this design is the use of an obtuse angled triangle, which has one of the three interior angles at more than 90°. Because this triangle is not symmetrical, the entire shape needs to be drawn to make the template. Make sure that your template paper is longer than necessary, so that the triangle can fully extend (see the cutting diagram below). Use the knee lift or hover feature on your sewing machine to making pivoting easier. Obtuse Triangle is an asymmetrical design, so mirror image marking will be necessary for block-based continuous quilting. Note that there are two different cutting diagrams depending on the version you select.

Design Variations   The focal point position as well as the use of different obtuse angles, creates different designs. Version 1 doesn't work as a continuous design since the interesting parts are cut off when it is confined to a block. Try rotating other triangles to see how the design changes.

VERSION 1

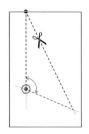 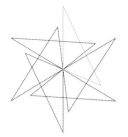 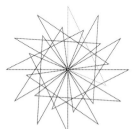 

Cutting Diagram for Versions 1 and 2

VERSION 2

 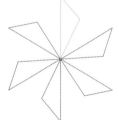 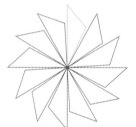 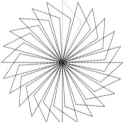 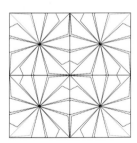

Circle

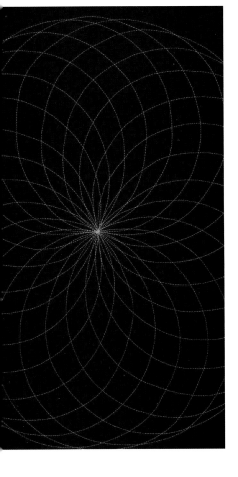

Sample Design Size   18″ in diameter

Template Length   9″

Marking Tool   Compass

Tips   The Circles are symmetrical, so draw the template on the fold.

Adjusting the Difficulty   Circles can be challenging to quilt, especially when there are many rotations. Reduce the number of rotations or increase the size of the Circle to make this design easier to execute accurately.

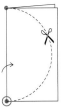

Cutting Diagram

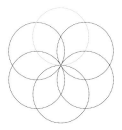

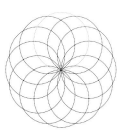

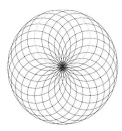

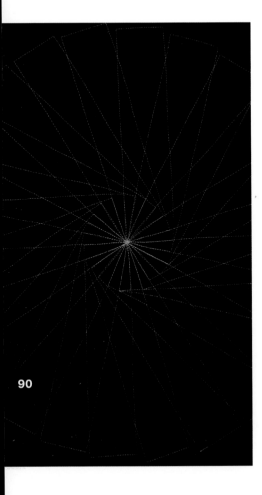

Rectangle

Sample Design Size 18″ in diameter

Template Length 9″

Marking Tool Ruler

Tips Since a Rectangle is symmetrical, you could draw the design on the fold to make the template, but a rectangle is easy to draw and cut as a single shape. Use the knee lift or hover feature on your machine to make pivoting easier. Because the placement of the focal point is offset, mirror-image marking will be necessary for block-based, continuous quilting. You will be retracing existing lines of quilting near the center, but this enhances the center by making the lines even bolder. With retracing, it can be easy to lose your place, so I recommend quilting one Rectangle at a time, systematically progressing around the circle to avoid getting lost in the design.

Design Variations Vary the width of the Rectangle or move the focal point to create new designs.

90

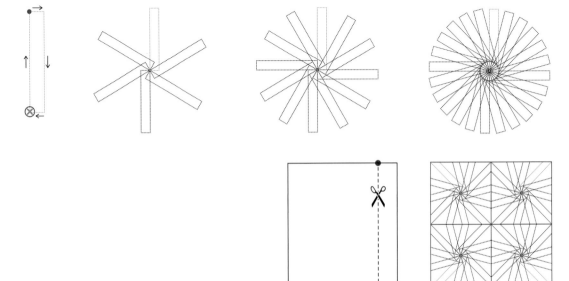

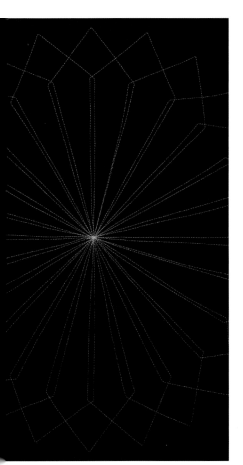

Elongated Diamond Version

Sample Design Size   18″ in diameter

Template Length   9″

Marking Tool   Ruler

Tips   The Elongated Diamond is symmetrical, so draw the design on the fold to make the template. Use the knee lift or hover feature on your machine to make pivoting easier. The design is symmetrical, so regular marking is used for block-based continuous quilting.

Adjusting the Difficulty   The thinner the diamond, the easier it will be to quilt since the pivot angle is reduced.

Design Variations   Different focal point locations create different designs. Adjust the pivot angle on the two side angles or adjust the length of the lines to create other variations.

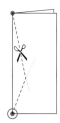

Cutting Diagram for both versions

VERSION 1

VERSION 2

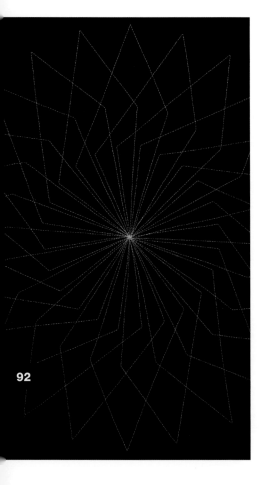

Skewed Parallelogram

Sample Design Size   18″ in diameter

Template Length   9″

Marking Tool   Ruler

Tips   Because of the asymmetry of the Skewed Parallelogram, the entire shape needs to be drawn to create a template and mirror image marking is necessary for block-based continuous quilting. Use the knee lift or hover feature on your machine to make pivoting easier.

Design Variations   Try a regular parallelogram, alter the sides to different angles or change the focal point to create variations of this design.

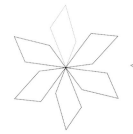
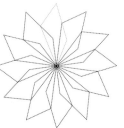

Cutting Diagram

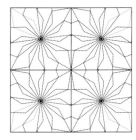

Elongated Pentagon

Sample Design Size   18″ in diameter

Template Length   9″

Marking Tool   Ruler

Tips   The Elongated Pentagon is symmetrical, so draw the shape on the fold. Use the knee lift or hover feature on your machine to make pivoting easier. Because of the symmetry of Version 1, regular marking will work for block-based continuous quilting. Due to the focal point placement in Version 2, the quilting is asymmetrical, so mirror-image marking is necessary for block-based continuous quilting. There may be some retracing of previously stitched lines near the center of this design. This thread buildup will enhance the center by making the lines even bolder. When retracing, it can be easy to lose your place when quilting. Quilt one shape at a time progressing around the circle to avoid getting lost in the design.

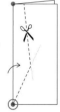

Cutting Diagram

Design Variations   Different focal point positions can create design variations. Change the width of the pentagon, the depth of the angles, or the length of the lines to create other variations.

VERSION 1

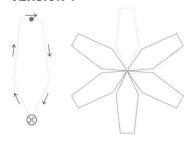 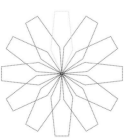 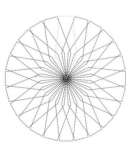 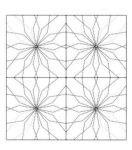

VERSION 2

  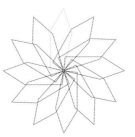  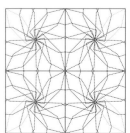

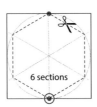

Regular Hexagon

Sample Design Size   18″ in diameter

Template Length   9″

Marking Tool   Compass and interval tool with 6 intervals

Tips   Mark the design as accurately as possible and be aware that the quilting lines will overlap in the center. This enhances the center by making the stitched lines even bolder, but it can be easy to lose your place when quilting. Quilt one shape at a time progressing around the circle to avoid getting lost in the design. Use the knee lift or hover feature on your machine to make pivoting easier.

Adjusting the Difficulty   Irregular Hexagons (see the facing page) are easier to quilt since the lines won't overlap.

Design Variations   The Regular Hexagon doesn't work as a continuous block-based design, but overlapping the design creates an intriguing variation. Experiment by drawing the design on paper or your computer. I created this version by overlapping the design.

Draw a circle with the diameter equal to the desired template length. Use the interval marking tool to divide the circle into six equal intervals. Connect the dots with lines to draw a hexagon. Cut out on the drawn lines.

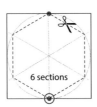

Cutting Diagram

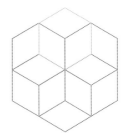

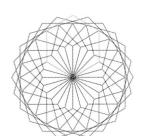

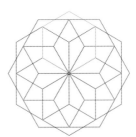

Irregular Hexagon

Sample Design Size   18˝ in diameter

Template Length   9˝

Marking Tool   Ruler

Tips   An Irregular Hexagon is symmetrical, so draw the design on the fold to make the template. Use the knee lift or hover feature on your machine to make pivoting easier. These are symmetrical, so regular marking also works for block-based continuous quilting.

Design Variations   Different focal point positions create design variations. Change the length of the lines or the size of the side angles to create other design options.

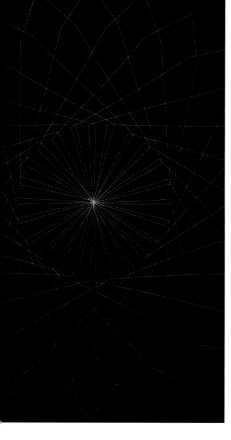

Cutting Diagram

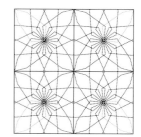

Random Hexagon

Sample Design Size   18″ in diameter

Template Length   9″

Marking Tool   Ruler, compass, and an interval tool with six interval markings.

Tips   Use the knee lift or hover feature on your machine to make pivoting easier. Random Hexagon is asymmetrical, so draw the entire shape to make the template. Both versions are asymmetrical, so mirror-image marking is necessary for block-based continuous quilting.

Design Variations   Different focal point positions create design variations. Draw any six-sided shape and experiment with the design possibilities.

Cutting Diagram

96

VERSION 1

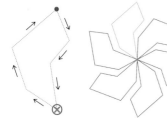 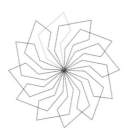 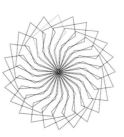 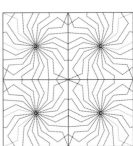

VERSION 2

   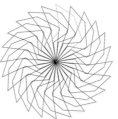 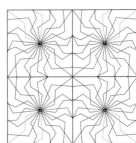

Curved Wedge

Sample Design Size 18″ in diameter

Template Length 9″

Marking Tool I used a 3″ circle template to mark the arc and a ruler to mark the lines.

Tips The Curved Wedge is symmetrical, so draw the shape on the fold to create the template. Use the knee lift or hover feature on your machine to make pivoting easier.

Design Variations There is no continuous design illustration for version 1 of the Curved Wedge. When confined to a block, the interesting features of this design are cut off. Version 2 is symmetrical, so regular marking works for block-based continuous quilting.

VERSION 1

  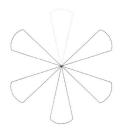 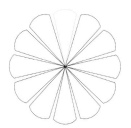 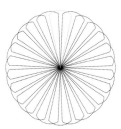

VERSION 2

    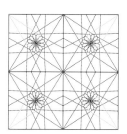

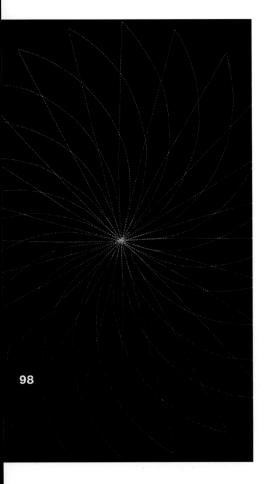

Curved Slice

Sample Design Size   18″ in diameter

Template Length   9″

Marking Tool   I used the edge of a 12″ circle template to mark the arc and a ruler to mark the line.

Tips   Use the knee lift or hover feature on your machine to make pivoting easier. Curved Slice is asymmetrical, so draw the entire shape to make the template. The design is asymmetrical, so mirror-image marking is necessary for block-based continuous quilting.

Adjusting the Difficulty   Reduce the depth of the curve to make quilting easier.

Design Variations   Increase or decrease the depth of the curve to change the amount of overlap and alter the look of the design.

Cutting Diagram

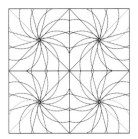

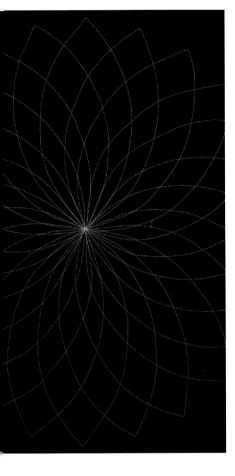

Leaf

Sample Design Size   18˝ in diameter

Template Length   9˝

Marking Tool   I used the edge of a 12˝ nested circle template to mark the arcs.

Tips   Use the knee lift or hover feature on your machine to make pivoting easier. Leaf is a symmetrical shape, so draw the shape on the fold to make the template. The design is also symmetrical, so regular marking will work for block-based continuous quilting.

Adjusting the Difficulty   The depth of the curve affects the difficulty of the design. Shallow curves are easier to quilt.

Design Variations   Vary the depth of the curve to create different design options. Wider leaves will overlap more for a different look.

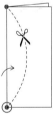

Cutting Diagram

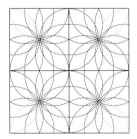

COMBINING DESIGNS

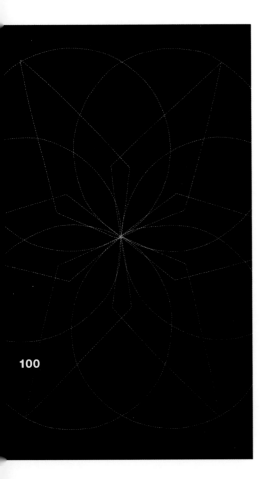

I played around a bit by combining two rotational designs to make a more intricate one. I also wanted to encourage your desire to play with design combinations and create your own. Playtime is valuable and may result in intriguing favorite new designs. When creating design combinations of your own, I encourage you to use fewer rotations because they will have plenty of complexity without the need for including an excessive number of them.

A Circle template with six rotations (page 89) plus an Elongated Diamond template (page 91) with six rotations equals Combined Design #1.

1. Mark a circle and divide it into 6 intervals.

2. Cut the Circle and Elongated Diamond templates to the same length as the radius of the circle from Step 1.

3. Mark the Circle design (see page 89) with 6 rotations and quilt.

4. Mark the Elongated Diamond (see page 91) with six rotations using the same center point as the Circles and quilt.

Using Rotational Designs

Rotational quilting with the walking foot is unexplored territory. I haven't been doing it for very long, but I'm hopeful that the publication of this book will result in rotational designs popping up all over. They are beautiful, elaborate and eye-catching, but are they practical and useful? It is important to know when and where rotational designs might be used to enhance your work and how to make them work for you.

These designs are perfect for projects like pillows, runners and small wall quilts where the amount of turning large pieces isn't a barrier to executing the quilting. Because they are based on circles, pieced curves and other rounded patchwork, they are natural candidates for rotational designs (fig. a). As all of the designs can be used in any size, consider supersized versions for medallion quilts or quilts with strong center focal points. Breaking a large quilt into smaller chunks with the quilt-as-you-go method (see page 162) is also a good way to support using rotational designs.

FILLING IN

Rotational designs quilted within circular shapes can be challenging because most of our piecing is made up of squares or rectangles. So, if a circular rotational design is quilted within a square, what can be done with the space around the design? The simplest way to fill these areas, is to emphasize the circular shape by quilting concentric circles around the design, and then echoing the arcs of the circle to fill in the remainder of the square.

Another option for filling in the square, is to make linear connections from the corners of the block to the rotational design, as I did with the Elongated Pentagon (see page 93) rotation. The red lines in Figure b indicate the lines I added.

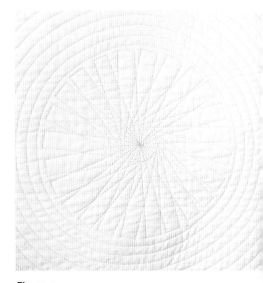

Figure a

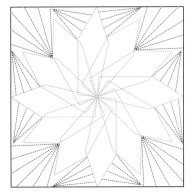

Figure b

Block-Based Continuous Designs

Rotational designs can also be used as block-based quilting designs. If the design is marked and confined within a block, the quilting can be much more continuous than if a full design is quilted within a circle. I shared how to mark within a block on page 72. When marking multiple blocks, it is important to place the interval tool in exactly the same position from block to block, as shown in Figure a.

Symmetrical shapes can be marked block-to-block and quilted edge-to-edge across the quilt. There will be some pivoting required during quilting, but there is no need to turn the whole quilt through the harp again and again. Notice in Figure b how the quilting path moves continuously from block to block across the quilt.

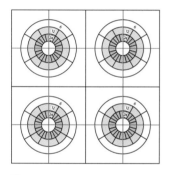

Figure a

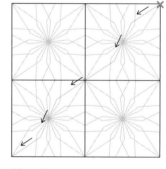

Figure b

TIP: Some symmetrical shapes will need to be marked with the mirror image if the focal point is placed off-center making the design asymmetrical. The Elongated Pentagon is a good example. The shape is symmetrical, but with the focal point in this position the rotational design will be asymmetrical.

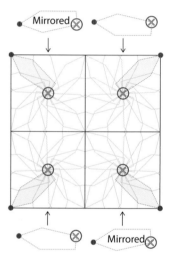

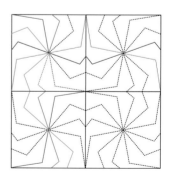

MARKING WITH MIRROR IMAGE FOR CONTINUOUS QUILTING

So what happens if the shape or the design is asymmetrical? These designs need to be marked with the regular design and the design's mirror image so they can be quilted continuously across a quilt. Mirror-image marking works well for asymmetrical linear or asymmetrical shape-based designs on block-based quilts. Notice in Figure c how each colored line of this linear rotation begins on the edge of the quilt and ends on the edge, making the design much easier to quilt because less turning is required. The colored lines aren't a rule for quilting, but simply to show how the lines connect and can be continuous. When quilting a quilt, move in whatever direction you need to connect

Figure c

lines across blocks and reduce the amount of turning and quilt manipulation required for the design.

Mirror imaging can also be used to make asymmetrical shape-based designs more continuous to quilt. The example I show here is of an Obtuse Triangle rotation. **(fig. d)**

To create a mirror image rotation, reflect the template to mark the mirror image. A reflection is a mathematical transformation. Don't worry, it's pretty simple, I promise. It is basically a 'flip' of a shape over an imaginary line of reflection. **(fig. e)**

Remember that when making templates, you will automatically create a mirror image template. It is important to mark your template indicating which side is the regular or mirror image version of the template so you don't get confused during the marking process. I recommend marking the top of the template as well. Better safe than sorry. Blocks can be marked alternating the regular design with the mirror image to create a design that can be quilted continuously **(fig. f)**. I label each block on the quilt with R for regular and M for mirror image before I do any marking on the quilt.

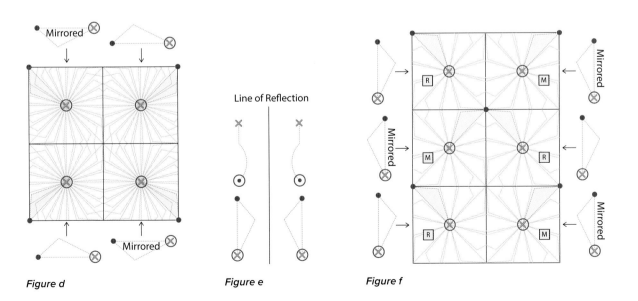

Figure d

Figure e

Figure f

MAKING AND USING CUSTOM STENCILS

Marking for continuous rotational quilting can be tedious. Creating custom stencils makes marking faster and easier. With a little investment of time up front, marking a bunch of blocks in a quilt will be much faster.

1. Cut a piece of Golden Threads Quilting Paper (see Resources page 175) or freezer paper the same size as the blocks in the quilt.

2. Mark the desired interval around the block and mark the design using the instructions on page 72 and 76. Use a thin-tipped pen to mark the desired rotational design onto the non-shiny side of the paper.

3. Unthread your sewing machine and install a large needle, such as a 100 topstitch needle.

4. Stitch the design on the paper. Essentially, you will be needle punching the design (fig. g). If using freezer paper, you can fuse multiple sheets of the paper together to make several stencils at one time. Having more than one stencil available is great for marking regular and mirror image designs.

5. Lightly spray the back of the stencil with basting spray.

6. Align the stencil on the block, making sure it is secure, and use Quilt Pounce Powder (see Resources page 175) to mark the design. Move the stencil to the next block and continue marking across the quilt. If the design is assymmetrical be sure to "flip" the stencil to use the mirror image in the appropriate blocks.

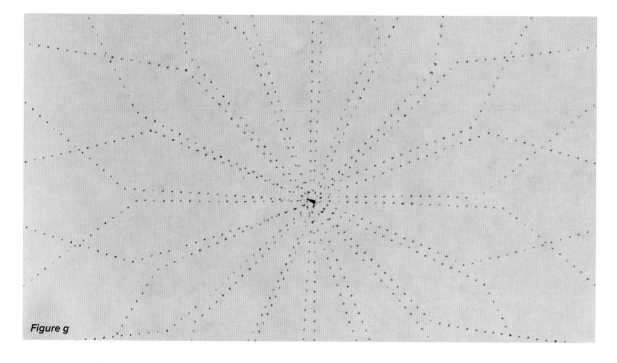

Figure g

SEND OFF

I hope you are as excited as I am about the designs in this chapter. Rotational designs add a unique flair to quilts and have the potential to highlight your piecing and elevate your quilts. Have fun, play and don't be intimidated by the intricacy of these designs or the amount of marking or turning required. You will never know what you can do unless you try. Add these designs to your quilting toolbox and always look for opportunities to rotate!

" New designs and variations of
the designs in WALK seemed to
just flow from my machine

VARIATIONS

I thought about writing WALK 2.0 a few months after WALK: Mastering Machine Quilting With Your Walking Foot was released. With the release of the first book, I was so jazzed about the possibilities of quilting with my walking foot, that new designs and variations of the designs in WALK seemed to just flow from my machine. This chapter contains a diverse collection of some of my favorite designs including point-to-point, curves, turning, radiating lines and even a new reverse design. I have increased the difficulty, tweaked designs to create new looks and added new designs as well. Many of the designs in this chapter require intensive marking and are challenging to quilt. I love a challenge and I hope you do too.

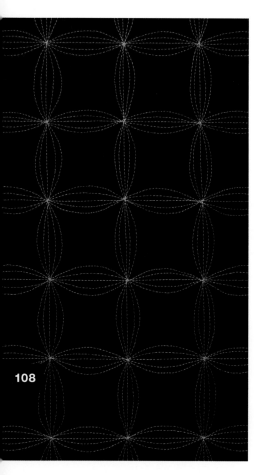

Double Orange Peel

The Double Orange Peel is a variation of the Orange Peel design. Adding additional curves makes this design a perfect complement to quilts that are pieced with identical finished squares and ups the density and complexity of the design.

1. Starting at the top center, Channel Quilt (see page 21) across the entire quilt top using a 2½″ interval. Rotate the quilt 180° and Channel Quilt to fill in the opposite side. Rotate the quilt 90° and repeat to create a grid.

2. On each vertical quilted line, mark dots a scant ½″ away from either side of the midpoint of each grid line, or mark the arcs. The edge of a small circle template works well for marking these.

3. Beginning on the center vertical line, quilt in an S-Curve motion from intersection to intersection using the marked dots or curves as your guide for the depth of the curve. **(fig. a)**

TIP: The grid should be in proportion to the distance marked from the grid lines. For larger grids, the marks can be further from the line. For example, on a 4″ grid the marks would be a generous ½″ out from the line. If you are unsure, test the distances by drawing a test square and a few arcs.

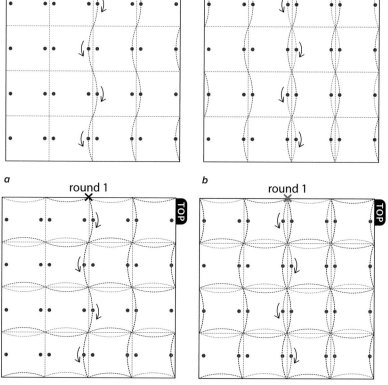

4. Slide the quilt back through the harp and repeat Step 2 for the opposite side of the line. **(fig. b)**

5. Repeat Steps 3-4 to complete the remainder of the vertical lines on the right half of the quilt. Rotate the quilt 180° and repeat Steps 2-4 to complete the left side of the quilt. **(figs. c & d)**

6. For round 2, again beginning at the center vertical line, echo another set of S-Curves about ⅛″ away from the previously quilted arcs across the right side of the quilt. It is easier to quilt these lines without marking since the previous line can act as a guide. Feel free to mark this second set of curves if preferred. If you aren't marking, remember that 'where-you-look-is-where-you-quilt'. **(figs. e & f)**

7. Rotate the quilt 180° and repeat Step 6 to finish the left side of the quilt. Rotate the quilt 90° and repeat to finish quilting the second set of curves in the opposite direction to complete the design. **(figs. g & h)**

TIP: The Double Orange Peel can also be quilted on a diagonal grid for a different look.

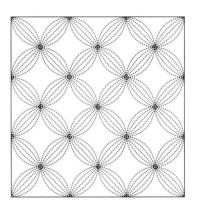

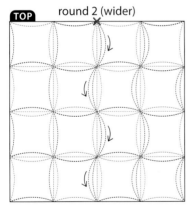

e

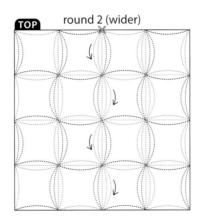

f

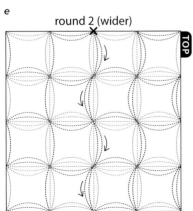

g

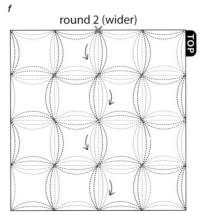

h

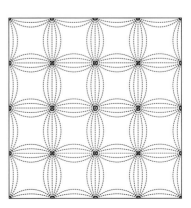

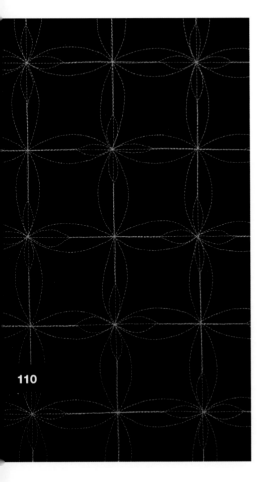

Flower in Orange Peel

Flower in Orange Peel is another variation of the Orange Peel. Instead of adding additional arcs, I added detail to the inside of the design. With a bit of retracing over already quilted lines and small S-Curves, delicate flowers appear at every other intersection to add charm to the design.

1. Starting at the top center, Channel Quilt (see page 21) across the entire quilt top using a 3″ interval. Rotate the quilt 180° and Channel Quilt to fill in the opposite side. Rotate the quilt 90° and repeat to create a grid.

2. On each vertical line, mark dots ½″ away from either side of the midpoint of each grid line, or mark the full arcs. **(fig. a)**

3. Repeat Steps 3-4 from the Double Orange Peel (see page 108) to create round 1 of the design. **(fig. b)**

4. Mark a dot at the mid point of the grid lines on each vertical line. Beginning at the center vertical line, quilt down the line retracing the previously quilted line. Stopping at the first dot, pivot and quilt a small S-Curve through the intersection and to the next dot. Continue quilting down the line to the next dot and repeat this pattern. **(fig. c)**

TIP: The edge of a small circle template works well for marking. Remember to mark in proportion to the size of the grid.

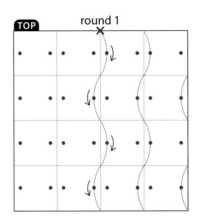

a

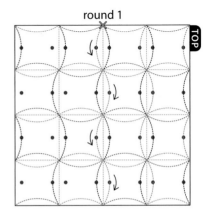

b

5. Slide the quilt back through the harp and repeat Step 4 to quilt the opposite side of the line. (fig. d)

6. Repeat Steps 4-5 on every other vertical line across the right side of the quilt. (fig. e)

7. Rotate the quilt 180° and repeat Steps 4-5 to complete the left side of the quilt. (fig. f)

8. Rotate the quilt 90° and complete the quilting in the opposite direction to complete the design.

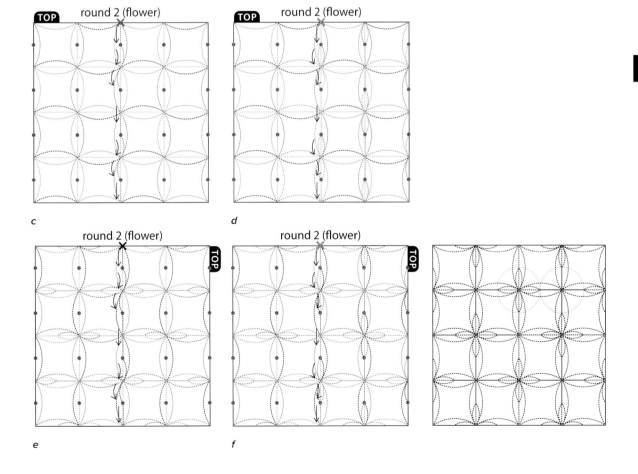

c

d

e

f

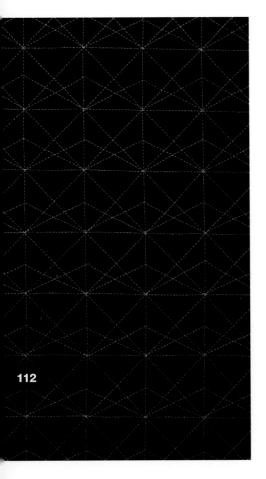

Intersecting Boomerangs

I did several boomerang designs in **WALK** and I've done several more variations since. I decided to show you my favorite, **Intersecting Boomerangs**. It is very easy to quilt with very little marking, but it looks complex and has a great retro vibe. **Intersecting Boomerangs is a grid-based design. Most of the design is quilted using the seam guide so there is very little marking.**

1. Starting at the top center, Channel Quilt (see page 21) across the entire quilt top using a 2″ interval. Rotate the quilt 180° and Channel Quilt to fill in the opposite side. Rotate the quilt 90° and repeat to create a grid.

2. Quilt diagonal lines through each square of the grid, in both directions. **(figs. a & b)**

3. Mark a dot midway between each horizontal grid line.

4. Beginning at a horizontal line nearest the center, quilt intersection-to-point-to-intersection forming an Elongated Diamond shape. **(fig.c)**

112

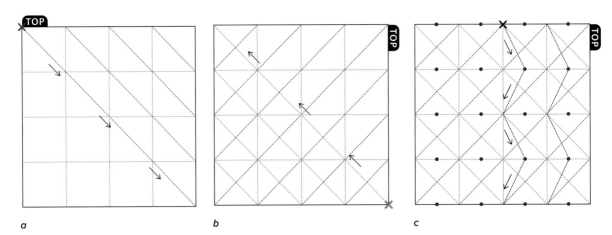

a　　　　　*b*　　　　　*c*

5. Move to the next horizontal line intersection. Drop the needle at the grid intersection and align the seam guide with the previously quilted line. Quilt point-to-point to finish one side of the quilt.

6. Rotate the quilt 180° to finish quilting point-to-intersection-to-point on the other side.

7. Go back to the marked point to the right of the intersection from Step 4, in the opposite direction. (fig. d)

8. Move to the next horizontal dot and use the seam guide to quilt point-to-point across the next row, aligning the seam guide with the previously quilted line. Repeat this process to finish one side of the quilt.

9. Rotate the quilt 180° and finish the design on the other side.

113

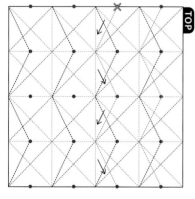

d

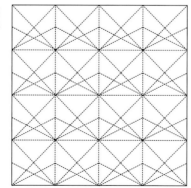

Mystic Rose

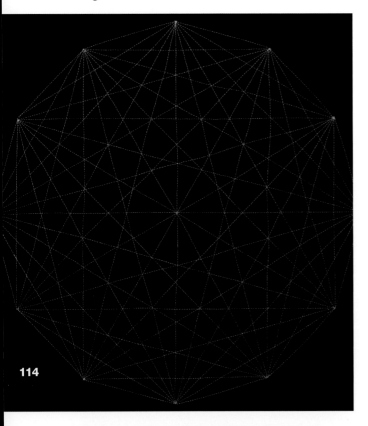

I discovered the Mystic Rose when I was researching linear geometric designs. It is created by connecting points equally spaced around a circle. Lines are drawn from each point on the circle to every other point around the circle. The intersections of the lines create a dynamic texture. Depending on the number of intervals the circle is divided into, the design can be challenging to mark so use a fine-tipped marking tool, like the Sewline pencil (see page 175), to make seeing each line easier. A single Mystic Rose can be quilted almost continuously with lots of turning or line-by-line with lots of starting and stopping. The method you choose should depend on the size of your quilt and the position of the design.

1. If you don't have pieced circles in your quilt, use a compass or a circle template and draw a circle. The size will be determined by the location of the design on the quilt.

2. Decide on the number of divisions for the circle. My sample is divided into 12. Mark the intervals on the circumference of the circle using an interval marking tool (see page 174) and marking instructions in the Rotational Designs chapter.

3. Choose a mark from Step 2 and draw lines from it to every other mark on the circle (fig. a). Repeat on an adjacent mark.

4. Beginning at the first marked point, drop the needle, pull up the bobbin thread and secure it using the tiny stitch method on page 87. Quilt from point-to-point around the circle, following the marked lines until all of the lines are quilted. (figs. b-e)

5. When you reach the starting point, stop, secure and clip the thread. Repeat Steps 3-4, pivot at each point on the circle until all of the marked lines are quilted. Secure with tiny stitches at the end of the line of quilting. (fig. f)

6. Continue marking and quilting two points at a time until all of the points are connected. (fig. g)

- -

TIP: Check the design carefully to make sure all of the lines are quilted. If you missed a line, quilt from point-to-point on the line making sure to secure with tiny stitches at the beginning and end of each line.

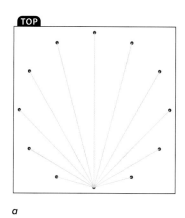

a

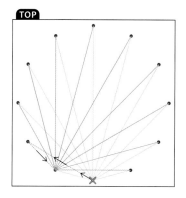

b

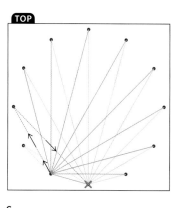

c

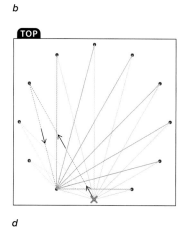

d

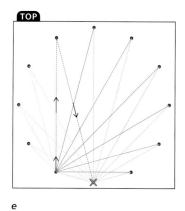

e

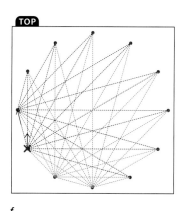

f

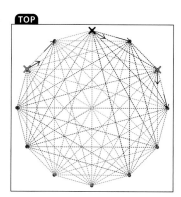

g

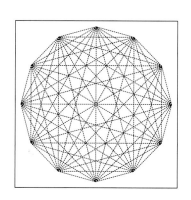

FILLER IDEAS

Mystic Rose fits well in pieced circles, but in blocks it is important to fill in the area around the circle too. To do this, here are a couple of great ideas to try. The first is an echoing of the outer lines of the design. In this example, Mystic Rose could also be quilted in the center of the quilt and the echoing could extend to the edges of the quilt.

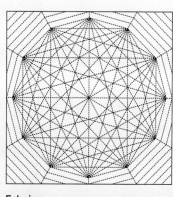

Echoing

Another option is to add additional sets of radiating lines to connect Mystic Rose to the edge of the block or quilt. If you are using this variation in multiple blocks, it is easy to connect the designs seamlessly.

Repeated Radiating Lines x4

Mystic Rose Variation

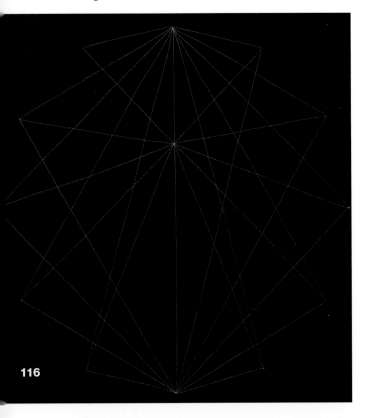

I created this variation of the Mystic Rose design for those of you who want a less dense but still distinctive design. The Mystic Rose Variation focuses on lines from two opposing points on a circle with a few lines added to create a center focal point. It also works well in repeated blocks with only a few added lines to create a cohesive design.

1. If you don't have pieced circles in your quilt, use a compass or a circle template and draw a circle. The size will be determined by the location of the design on the quilt.

2. Mark 12 intervals on the outer circumference of the circle using an interval marking tool (see page 174) and marking instructions on page 72 of the Rotational Designs chapter. (fig. a)

3. Starting with the top and bottom intervals, mark lines from these two points to all the other points on the circle. (fig. b)

4. Beginning at the dot on the bottom of the circle (indicated here with a blue X), quilt along the marked lines following the path indicated by the arrows (fig. c) returning to the starting point.

5. Repeat Step 4 to quilt the second path of quilting following the path indicated here in red. (fig. d)

6. Repeat Step 5 to complete two more paths of quilting on all of the marked lines.

7. Mark the additional lines indicated in Figure e and quilt along the marked lines following the path indicated by the arrows making sure to secure your stitching at the beginning and end of the lines.

8. Repeat Step 7 marking and quilting the additional sets of lines indicated in Figures f and g to complete the design.

a

b

c

d

e

f

g

The Mystic Rose Variation works well when repeated in blocks. Here, I rotated the rose 45° and placed four blocks together with the bottom of the blocks pointing towards the center. That 4-block set is repeated four times to create this design.

I added a few additional lines to the design to make continuous quilting of the lines easier.

117

This is a massive investment in marking and quilting. To reduce the time it would take to mark this quilt, make a needle punched stencil (see page 104). With a marking stencil in hand and the ability to quilt more continuously with less turning and manipulation, this design is totally achievable.

Radiating Concentric

The Radiating Concentric design is a combination of two designs in _WALK_. I love the three-dimensional quality that it creates, but what really thrills me is what happens when it is quilted block-to-block. Because the top has to be turned through the harp for each block, it is a challenge to quilt but yields a captivating result.

1. Mark the center of the quilt with a dot. Center a 2″ square around the dot. Draw two diagonal lines corner-to-corner across the area that bisects the square.

2. Quilt three angled lines from the edges of the corners of the quilt or block to the edges of the drawn square. Make sure to secure your stitches at the start and end if quilting using the tiny stitch method (see page 87). The remaining diagonal line will be quilted as you travel down it to move from one concentric square to the next.

3. At the un-quilted corner, mark the EFNI (see page 10) or your chosen interval down the un-stitched diagonal line (fig. a). If you plan to use the stitch counting method in Step 4, you only need to mark the first dot.

4. Beginning at the corner of the square with the un-stitched diagonal, drop the needle on the corner, pull up the bobbin thread and secure using the tiny stitch method. Quilt around the square following the marked line from Step 1. When you reach the starting corner, pivot and quilt down the diagonal line to the next marked dot from Step 3. Count the number

---

TIP: When quilted as a single design, the area near the center will be the most challenging but the quilting gets easier as the design moves out towards the edges.

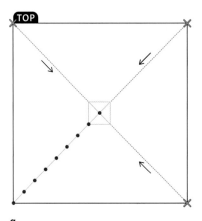

a

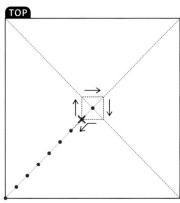

b

of stitches on the diagonal it takes to reach the marked dot. If you do this, you can use that stitch count for each round of the concentric squares. Pivot and align the edge of the walking foot or set the seam guide using the previously quilted line to set the interval. **(fig. b)**

5. Continue quilting around the square **(fig. c)**, pivoting at the diagonal lines, keeping the edge of the walking foot or the seam guide aligned with the previously quilted square. When you reach the point on the square where you began, pivot and quilt down the diagonal the same distance as in Step 4. **(fig. d)**

6. Use the Interval Tool B (see page 174). Mark 24 intervals around the block (see page 72). Mark the radiating lines, except those on either side of the vertical and horizontal line.

7. Quilt the marked lines from the center dot to the outside edge of the block or quilt to complete the design. **(fig. e)**

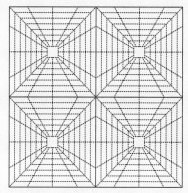

This is a symmetrical design, so multiples work well together and connect seamlessly.

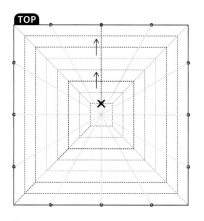

c

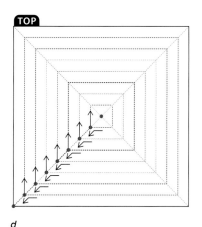

d

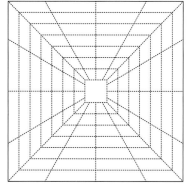

e

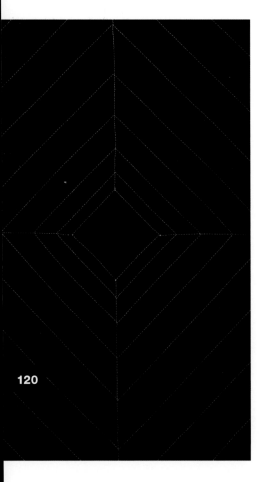

120

Tunnel Concentric

Tunnel Concentric is another variation on traditional concentric quilting, but changes the intervals between the lines as they move outward. The perpendicular lines are used to mark the pivot points, but also contribute to the effect of this design. Determine the number of interval changes and the number of intervals based on the size of the design. A larger area can handle more and larger intervals. On my sample I began with a ½″ interval and increased it by adding three more stitches on the horizontal line after the first round and reset the seam guide to the new interval.

1. Mark the center of the quilt with a dot and use it to center a 2″ on-point square around it. Draw two perpendicular lines across the quilt that bisect the square.

2. Quilt three lines from the middle of the edges of the area to be quilted to the edges of the drawn square (fig. a). Make sure to secure your stitches at the start and end if quilting using the tiny stitch method (see page 87). The remaining line will be quilted when traveling from one concentric square to the next.

3. Along the un-quilted line, mark a dot from the corner of the quilted square to the first desired interval. (fig. b)

4. Drop the needle on the corner of the inner square indicated here with a red X, pull up the bobbin thread and secure using the tiny stitch method. Quilt in a clockwise movement around

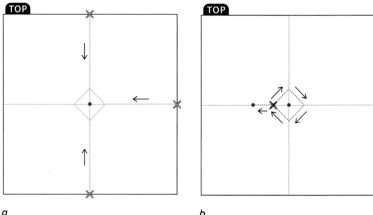

a　　　　　　　　　　　　b

the square until you are back at the starting corner. Pivot and quilt down the un-quilted marked line to the dot that marks the first interval (fig. c). Count the number of stitches it takes to reach that marked point. Pivot and align the edge of the walking foot or set the seam guide using the previously quilted line as a guide. Use this stitch count to establish a consistent travel interval for each time around the concentric square.

5. Continue quilting around the square, pivoting at the lines from Step 1, keeping the edge of the walking foot or the seam guide aligned with the previously quilted square. Quilt as many rounds as desired and secure the stitching at the end.

6. To change the interval, drop the needle after completing the last square from the first interval. Mark a dot along the un-quilted line at the second chosen interval. Begin quilting where you dropped the needle and continue quilting around the square. Quilt as many rounds as desired at the second interval. Secure the stitching at the end.

7. Repeat Step 6 to set a new interval and quilt another set of rounds. Quilt as many rounds as desired changing the interval as many times as desired.

8. When you can no longer quilt a complete round, echo the lines in each corner out to the edge to complete the design.

Adding additional radiating lines can make the Tunnel Concentric even more three-dimensional. Follow Step 7 of the Radiating Concentric design (see page 118) to add additional lines to create this variation.

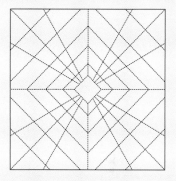

The Tunnel Concentric concepts can also be applied to other shapes like circles, rectangles, hexagons and triangles. The marking for each shape will be different for the traveling line and turning points though.

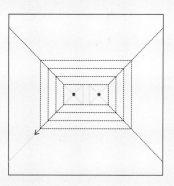

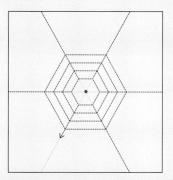

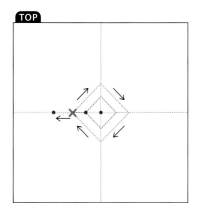

c

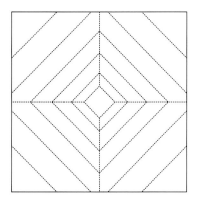

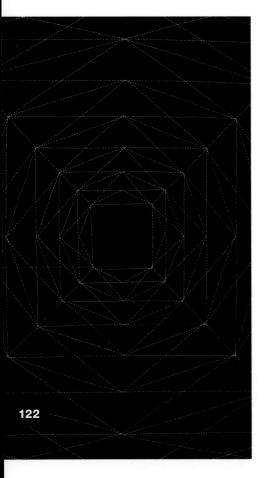

Tunneling Triangles

Tunneling Triangles is an extension of the Tunnel Concentric (see page 120). The concentric squares provide the base for this design. Point-to-point lines are quilted within each round of the squares using the radiating lines as the pivot points. When quilting this design, it feels much like spiraling except with straight lines. The quilting is challenging near the center but it gets easier as you move towards the edges of the quilt. The inner lines can typically be quilted using the "where-you-look-is-where-you-quilt' technique with no initial marking. As the points get farther apart, you may need to begin marking the lines and quilt following them depending on your comfort level with this technique. My sample is quilted with the concentric squares getting a bit further apart with each round.

1. Follow Steps 1-6 to quilt the Tunnel Concentric design (see page 120) but in Step 2, quilt only two of the diagonals from the corners of the inner square. Traveling from square to square while quilting the Tunnel Concentric will create the third diagonal. The fourth diagonal will be quilted when traveling. Figure a shows the completed Tunnel Concentric and the red X shows the starting point for the Tunneling Triangles design.

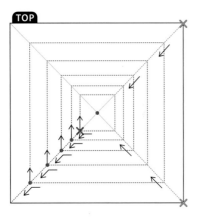

a

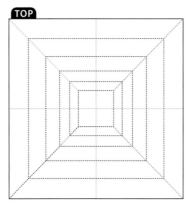

b

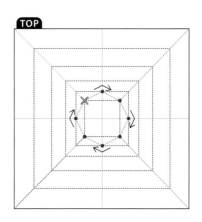

c

2. Draw a vertical and horizontal line across the quilt that bisects the center square. These lines will serve as additional pivot points for the design. **(fig. b)**

3. Drop the needle on the green X, secure and quilt corner-to-intersection around the square as shown. **(fig. c)**

4. When you reach the starting point, quilt corner-to-intersection around the square again, but from the corner of the square to the midpoint in the next square and back to the corner of the square again **(fig. d)**. Repeat this pattern around the square, back to the start point.

5. From the start point, quilt over the marked diagonal line to reach the corner of the next square indicated here with the black X. Repeat the process in Steps 3-4. When you reach the start point, quilt on the diagonal to reach the corner of the next square. **(fig. e)**

6. Repeat Steps 3-5 for each concentric square to complete the design. In the outer squares you may need to mark the point-to-point lines if they are too far apart to quilt without marking.

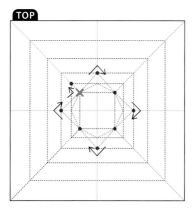

d

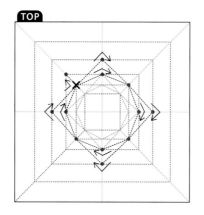

e

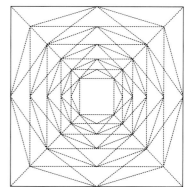

Reverse Vines

In *WALK*, I shared an entire chapter of reverse designs. Reverse Vines is a curved adaptation of Twigs from that chapter. When I mentioned to a student that I was experimenting with reverse curves, she went for it and Reverse Vines was born. This is a free-flowing design with lots of movement and it is fairly simple to execute. If you've never quilted in reverse, review the information on page 22. Practice a few times on a sample and you'll be ready to give it a try on a quilt.

1. Roughly near the center of the quilt, mark or place painter's tape vertically top to bottom. Mark or tape a parallel line about 8″ to 12″ away from the first line, depending on the width of the quilt. These lines help keep the quilting in the next step from veering too far away from the vertical.

2. Attach the seam guide and set the interval for 2″. Beginning at the top about 2″ to the right of the tape or marked line, quilt flowing gentle curves to the bottom of the quilt. Use the seam guide to keep the curves about the same distance apart. Try not to echo the previously quilted line exactly, but there needs to be enough space between the lines to add the 'leaves'. Quilt wavy curved lines from top to bottom to fill the right side of the quilt. Remove the tape.

3. Rotate the quilt 180° and repeat Steps 1-2 to fill the left side with wavy curves. For a denser design, add another wavy line between each of the already quilted lines. **(fig. a)**

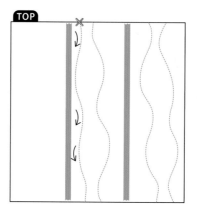

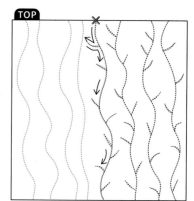

a   b

4. Beginning at the top of the center quilted line, quilt over the top of the previous line of stitching about 4″ to 6″, then stop with the needle down. Pivot and aim to the right. Hold the reverse button on your machine and stitch in reverse 6 to 8 stitches along the previously quilted line. Stitch forward, retracing the line and stopping when you reach the vine again. If the lines curve a bit, great! Pivot and continue stitching down the vine until you come to your next 'leaf'. **(fig. b)**

5. Continue quilting down the vine, but this time pivot to the left and stitch in reverse on the opposite side of the vine. Repeat this process all the way down the vine. How often you stop to reverse is up to you.

6. Repeat Steps 4-5 to add 'leaves' to all the curved lines on the right side of the quilt.

7. Rotate the quilt 180°. To add leaves to the remainder of the curved lines, quilt the leaves forward first and retrace in reverse to keep the leaves facing in the proper direction on the vine. Quilt leaves on all of the remaining curved lines to complete the design. **(fig. c)**

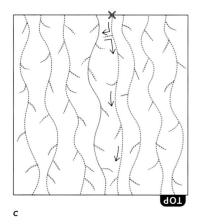

c

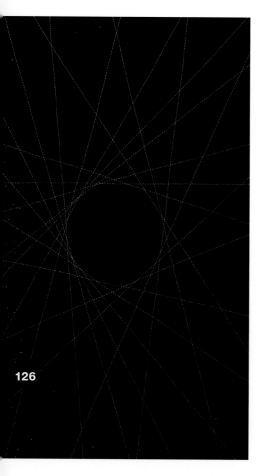

Tangent

Tangent is a geometric design that I first saw used by Dan Rouse from California and it inspired the design of one of my favorite quilts, *Dancing on the Table with Dan*. It proves that quilting doesn't always need to be difficult to be special. In geometry, a tangent is a straight line that touches a circle or curve without crossing it. Outside of geometry, tangent also means a completely different thought or action, which really fits this design. Let's go off on a tangent and quilt something totally different.

1. Using a circle template or a compass, draw a circle. The circle in my sample is 4″ in diameter. The size of the circle will depend on where the design is located on the quilt top and whether you will be doing additional quilting in the circle.

2. Tangent needs to be quilted within a confined area that is determined prior to quilting. My sample is 20″ square.

3. Draw a line from one edge of the defined area to another, being sure it touches the circumference of the circle at one point. Continue drawing lines surrounding the circle until you achieve the density you desire. (figs. a & b)

4. Quilt on the drawn lines. If the lines are located within the quilt, be sure to secure at the start and end of each line with the tiny stitch method (see page 87).

5. Look at your design. If you feel it needs additional density, draw and quilt additional lines.

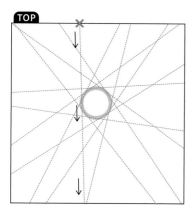

a

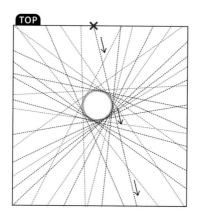

b

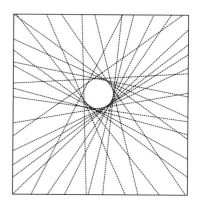

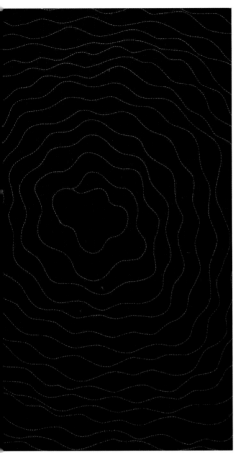

Rose Spiral

Gently curved lines can do amazing things and in the case of the Rose Spiral they create the impression of the interior of a rose. I was teaching traditional spiraling and one of my students was struggling to echo a circle. Her spiral was wobbling all over the place. After chatting with her, we decided that she had invented the wobbly spiral and when I tried it at home, I understood how difficult it was. This was a reminder that it can often be possible to turn a mistake into a strength! Marking the tightest part of this spiral first will help you get started. Also, try not to slip into an echoing pattern. Aim to keep the wobbles unique as you move from the center outward. The quilting gets easier as you move away from the center and there is less quilt in the harp, but wobbling is still a challenging quilting technique.

1. Use a compass or a circle template to mark a 3″ or 4″ diameter circle. Draw a curved wobbly pattern around the circle, keeping the curves as gentle as possible. (fig. a)

2. Drop the needle on the start point and secure using the tiny stitch method (see page 87). Quilt on the wobbly marked line. Near the end, shift a little to continue around the circle in a gentle wobbling pattern. Try to keep fairly consistent spacing between the quilting using the edge of the foot or a seam guide to help. Variations are what make this design charming.

3. Continue quilting until reaching the edge of the area (fig. b). Fill in any corners by quilting wobbly lines out to the corners.

127

- -
TIP: Consider using a decorative stitch to simulate a wobble. Let the stitch do the work! If they are available on your machine decorative stitches like the serpentine or scallop work well.

a

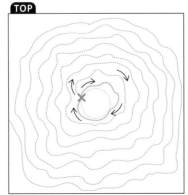

b

Starfield

Starfield is a combination of a grid and point-to-point work. It creates beautiful stars and even the illusion of circles. The design is intensive. It requires a good bit of marking which is made easier by using a square template.

1. Starting at the top center, Channel Quilt (see page 21) across one side of the quilt top using a 1½″ interval. Rotate the quilt 180° and repeat to fill in the opposite side. Rotate the quilt 90° and repeat to create a grid.

2. Locate the center intersection of four squares on the grid. Center a 1½″ square template on the intersection and trace an on-point square. Skip one grid line and mark another square continuing across and down the quilt in this pattern. (fig. a)

3. Quilt a diagonal line intersecting the grid squares to fill in the right side (fig. b). Rotate 180° and quilt all the diagonals to

---

TIP: Cut a 1½″ square (or a square the same size as your chosen grid interval) from cardboard to use as a marking template. The size of the marking square should be the same as the grid squares in the design.

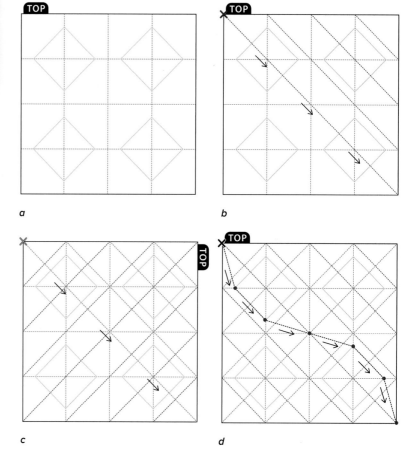

a

b

c

d

fill in the left side. Repeat to quilt the diagonals in the opposite direction to complete the diagonal grid. (fig. c)

4. Start at the top left intersection marked with a green X in Figure d and quilt point-to-point from the intersection, to the corner of the marked square, down the side of the square then from the corner of the square to the next intersection. Continue quilting this pattern diagonally down the quilt. Slide the quilt back through the harp and repeat for the opposite side. (fig. e)

5. Back at the top of the quilt, move over two intersections and repeat Step 4 to fill in the right side of the quilt. Rotate the quilt 180° and fill in the left side of the quilt. (figs. f & g)

6. Rotate the quilt 90 degrees and repeat Steps 4 and 5 to complete the design.

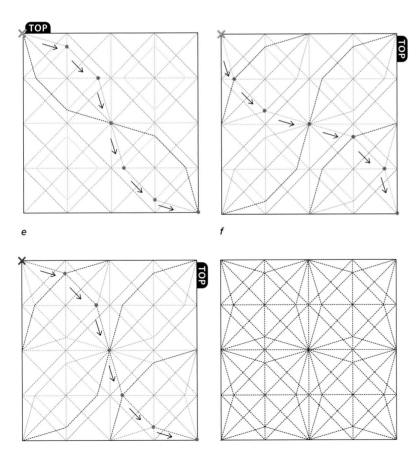

e

f

g

Tunneling Star

Tunneling Stars is another extension of the Tunnel Concentric design (see page 120) and is quilted the same way as the Tunneling Triangles design (see page 122) except additional radiating lines are quilted to add additional pivot points. As with the other concentric designs, the quilting is challenging near the center but gets easier as you move towards the edge of the quilt. The inner lines can typically be quilted using the 'where-you-look-is-where-you-quilt' technique and no marking. As the points get farther apart, you may need to mark the lines and quilt following the marked lines, depending on your comfort level with this technique. The sample is quilted with the concentric squares getting a bit further apart with each round.

1. Follow Steps 1-6 to quilt the Tunnel Concentric design (see page 120). In Step 2 of those directions, quilt only two of the diagonals from the corners of the inner square. Traveling from square to square while quilting the Tunnel Concentric will create the third diagonal. The fourth diagonal will be quilted when traveling to quilt this design. **(fig. a)**

2. Place Interval Marking Tool B (see page 174) in the center of the design. Tape or pin the tool to the quilt so it doesn't move. Use the marks on the tool and a ruler to draw lines, creating 16

130

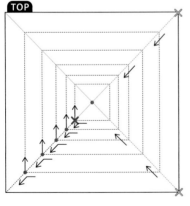

a

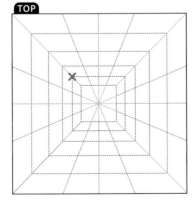

b

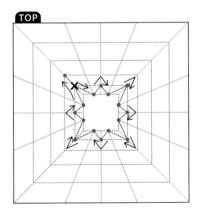

c

intervals. Be sure the lines on the tool align with the diagonals in the quilted Tunnel Concentric. Quilt all of the marked lines radiating from the edge of the center square to the edge of the quilt except one (fig. b). This is the traveling line for quilting point-to-point around the concentric ring. Make sure to secure the stitching at the start and end of each line if the line ends on the quilt top. These new lines will serve as additional pivot points. The completed Tunnel Concentric, the quilted lines and the start point for the Tunneling Stars design are shown in Figure c.

3. Drop the needle on the black X, secure, and quilt point-to-point around the central quilted square, marking if desired. (fig. c)

4. When you return to the start point, quilt down the un-quilted diagonal to reach the corner of the next square. Repeat the process in Step 3 to quilt point-to-point around the square. When you return to the start point again, quilt down the diagonal to reach the corner of the next square. (fig. d)

5. Repeat Steps 3-4 for each concentric square to complete the design. In the outer squares you may need to mark the point-to-point lines if they are too far apart to quilt without marking.

SEND OFF

I know this chapter is filled with an eclectic collection of designs. It's a good thing to have options and many of you have requested more complex and challenging designs to quilt. It is inspiring to know that you want to go further to develop your skills and quilt designs like these. Many of them require a good bit of investment of time and effort as all good things do.

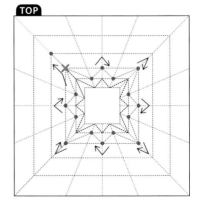

d

" **There are no quilting soul mates.**

QUILT AS DESIRED

HOW TO QUILT IT

I enjoy all the steps in quilt making: choosing fabrics, design, piecing, quilting and binding, but the most challenging part of the process is deciding how to quilt my top. Quilt as desired: that phrase makes my heart beat faster and creates a sense of dread every time I read it. How do I know what I desire? That statement nagged me with every quilt. It took years for me to figure out how to tackle the 'how do I quilt it?' question. At the end of my online and in-person walking foot quilting classes I invite the students to share their quilting dilemmas so that we can help each other with quilting advice. Students have taken that invitation to heart and over the last seven years I've looked at hundreds of quilt tops in all styles and offered advice and recommendations for quilting designs. I have listened to my students' suggestions and tried to see quilts through their eyes and learn from their ideas. I've also taken what I've learned about the elements and principles of design and applied that knowledge to their quilts. This knowledge and experience has helped me to hone my process and philosophy as well, which is what I'm sharing with you in this chapter. I hope the information, ideas, and example quilts will help you decide what you desire.

A Quilt is a Composition

The students in my quilting classes tell me that when it comes to how to quilt a quilt, I look at quilts differently from other people. I think what they mean is that for many quilters a quilt is composed of parts: pieces, blocks, sashing and borders and when it comes to quilting, they think of quilting designs in terms of those parts. Quilters who look at quilts that way ask questions like: What should I do in the blocks or on the border? What should I quilt in each of the squares? It's fine to view quilts as a set of parts, but it may yield different answers to the 'how do I quilt it?' question. Rather than looking at quilts in terms of their parts, I look at a quilt as a whole, as a composition. A composition in art is the thoughtful placement or arrangement of visual elements to create a whole. We put together parts to make a whole quilt and viewing it as a complete composition may help you see how the quilting can support or enhance the overall design. My goal when choosing a quilting design is to have the pieced design and quilting design merge into a cohesive composition. I tend to de-emphasize the quilting and sometimes let it play a lesser role in the composition, but even if you want the quilting to take a more prominent role in your quilts, the quilting should work with the piecing rather than interfering with or overwhelming it.

CHOMP

Chomp is matchstick quilted with areas of ⅛″ and areas of ¼″ interval lines. The differing intervals create shadows across the quilt which give the piece depth and interest. The verticality of the lines reinforces the proud, strong and stable nature of the design.

Quilting as a Design Element

Quilting is a powerful and multi-faceted design element. Walking foot quilting is composed primarily of lines. Lines are a fundamental design element in art and understanding the design principles around them may help you in your 'quilt as desired' dilemma.

VISUAL GRAMMAR OF LINES

Lines have a visual grammar. They can be vertical, horizontal, diagonal, curved, undulating, parallel, perpendicular, scattered, radiating, and can zig and zag and each type of line communicates a different message. Each of the different ways we put lines together conveys different meanings as well. Lines in combination create patterns and textures and different effects on your quilt. For example, parallel lines at equal intervals are orderly and static. Curved lines echoed at equal intervals create an orderly sense of movement while more randomly spaced and randomly curved lines will feel more wild and free. Spacing lines randomly is more dynamic and disorderly. When lines cross at right angles, the resulting grid is rational and conservative and maybe even a bit safe. Lines crossing at other angles can be more lively and spirited. Lines in combination will also create shadows and differences in value. Lines can draw the eye, create shape, divide, unify, and provide focus.

The information in the chart will help you understand the language of lines. Lines are a powerful tool for a quilter to master. We will explore the principles of line in detail and then apply them to quilting as a design layer.

HORIZONTAL	Horizontal lines are parallel to the horizon and evoke a calm, natural order and can be comforting and relaxing. Horizontal lines can't fall over and they accentuate width. Because of their calm stability they may also seem boring.
VERTICAL	Vertical lines are proud and strong and stand for stability, tradition and dignity. Vertical lines accentuate height, length and lack of movement, but they are filled with potential so they seem more interesting than horizontal lines. They can be both stately and seem rigid and unnatural.
CURVED	Curved lines move, change direction and can be unpredictable and playful. Curved lines can be both calm and energetic depending on the depth of the curve. Curves convey movement and flow; they can evoke the image of the human body and therefore give a soft natural, organic feeling.
DIAGONAL	Diagonal lines are active and full of potential and movement. They suggest directionality, movement, energy and excitement. Diagonal lines can bring life to quilts and direct the eye in an upward or downward direction. Diagonal lines may feel unbalanced and a bit out of control. Many diagonal lines in different directions can create the feeling of chaos. Often a diagonal line needs another diagonal in the opposite direction to feel more balanced.
RADIATING	Radiating lines are organized around a focal point and create a feeling of organization, regularity and balance. Radiating lines guide the eye and create movement either towards or away from the focal point.
ZIGZAG	Zigzag lines are a combination of diagonals in different directions. The abrupt change in direction is dynamic and exciting. Zigzag lines create a strong sense of movement and rhythm.
SPIRALING	Spiraling lines in both straight lines and curves imply movement either from or towards the center of the spiral. Spirals create a sense of flow and boundlessness.

WHAT CAN A QUILTING DESIGN DO FOR YOUR QUILT?

→ Add texture

→ Create unity or differentiate

→ Add, extend or enhance design elements

→ Emphasize or add a focal point

→ Create movement and flow

→ Take advantage of the pieced structure (define shapes)

→ Create a mood or feeling

→ Disappear and/or stabilize

Let's look at some of these in detail with some example quilts. Each of these quilts needed something provided by the quilting to complete an effective composition.

137

ADDING TO THE DESIGN

The Role of Quilting in a Composition

In addition to knowing the expressive quality of lines, knowing the role that quilting plays in a composition may help you decide what your quilt may need.

ADD TEXTURE

At its most basic, quilting adds texture to the quilt top. Texture stimulates the senses of sight and touch and can add interest and promote depth. When using lines to create texture, the possibilities are endless. It is important to consider the interval between quilting lines when creating textural quilting. Lines spaced at larger intervals will read more as a motif. With smaller intervals, lines will merge together and read as a texture. For example, when quilting a diagonal crosshatch, lines two inches apart will read as large diamonds whereas lines ½" apart will read as a diamond-like texture. Textural quilting can be a unifying element for sampler quilts with many different blocks or it can be used to unify areas of negative space in your quilts. One of my favorite textural quilting designs is crosshatching, since it is easy to quilt and there are endless variations. The Six Set Grid quilted on the Mid-Century House (opposite) creates a stunning texture showcased by the heavy-weight thread and bold color.

CREATE UNITY OR DIFFERENTIATION

Quilting can be used to unify disparate elements in a quilt and pull a quilt together into a more unified composition. A sampler quilt is a perfect example in which the quilting can pull a set of very different blocks together to create a unified whole. On a sampler quilt, choose an overall quilting design to create a background on which each block can sing. Quilting designs can unify blocks, sections or elements within a quilt like borders or sashing. So when you're looking to pull things together in your quilt, think quilting.

Quilting can also be used to differentiate similar elements within a composition by adding detail or texture to make each pieced element special. Varying quilting designs within a quilt draws the viewer's eye and creates interest and variety within a repetitive composition.

Quiet Geometry (opposite) is all about circles and the quilting is used to differentiate and unify. The rotational quilting gives each pieced circle its own unique identity and elevates the quilt to another level. The additional circular rotational quilting in the un-pieced areas repeats the pieced motif and strengthens the visual unity of this simple piece.

ADD, EXTEND OR ENHANCE DESIGN ELEMENTS

Sometimes the piecing is only the beginning of the design of a quilt. The quilting can be an equal partner with the piecing to create a cohesive composition. Many modern quilts have large areas of negative space that provide a canvas for adding, extending or enhancing the design elements in the piecing. Quilting lines may be extended from the piecing into the negative space. Shapes can be quilted echoing shapes in the piecing. Partial shapes in the piecing can be completed with quilting. Words can be quilted or made to appear using matchstick quilting. Quilting may be the magical element needed to take a quilt from ordinary to extraordinary.

The quilting on Rose and Thorn (opposite) is an integral part of the composition of this quilt. The quilt is an abstracted rose bush with the pieced elements representing the branches and thorns. The linear curves of the quilting intertwine and surround the pieced shapes creating softness and the impression of the rounded bush. Together the quilting and piecing create an effective composition.

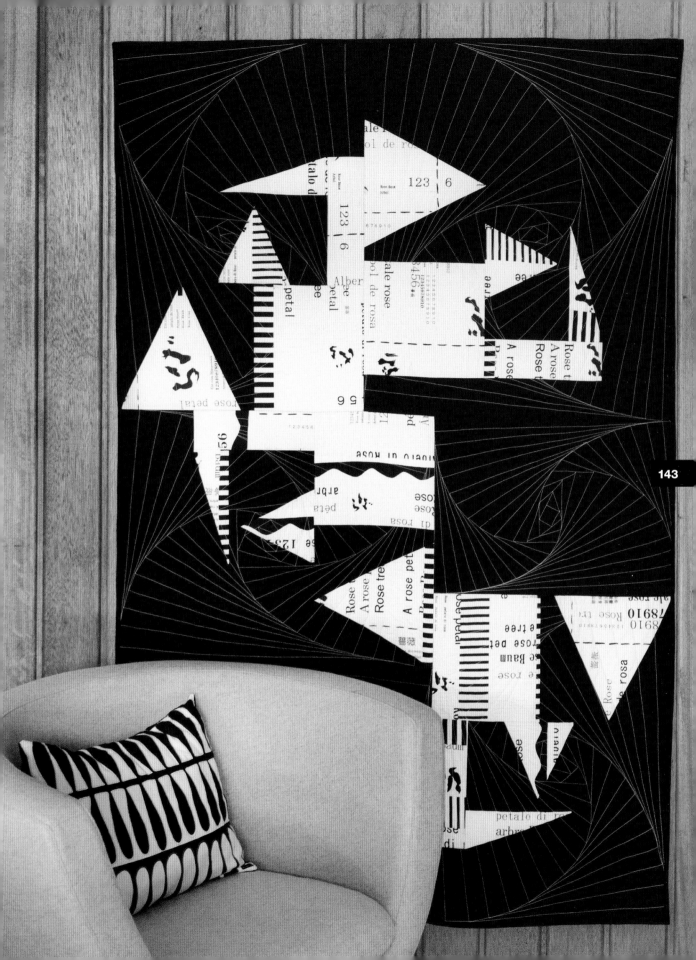

EMPHASIZE OR ADD A FOCAL POINT

When we put all that effort into piecing and quilting a quilt we want to draw folks into it. We want them to look closer and to see the work we've done. The focal point draws the eye of a viewer to the most important part or the area you want to highlight. Quilting lines can emphasize the focal point and act as leading lines or an easy path to follow to lead the viewer where you want them to look. Quilting lines can also create a focal point when there isn't one. For example when all the quilting lines meet in the center of a quilt, the eye is drawn to the center and the viewer will be drawn there too.

Jay's Star (opposite) is a rare seven pointed star design. I'm pretty proud of the twenty-one seams that come together at the center of this quilt. The quilting is designed to emphasize the unique piecing and draw the eye to that fabulous center. The pieced design naturally divides the quilt into seven sections so I took advantage of that structure and echoed in within each of the sections. The equally spaced lines create a calm, orderly feeling, but at the same time the v-shaped quilting draws the eye into the star and says 'look at me'.

CREATE MOVEMENT AND FLOW

Movement is a powerful design principle and can be used to guide a viewer's eye through a composition or to a focal point. Quilting lines can be used to create a sense of movement in your quilt. Curved lines, even very gentle curves are especially effective when used to add movement, softness and flow to a quilt. Observe the difference between the Starburst executed in straight lines and in gently curved lines.

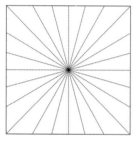
Starburst with Lines

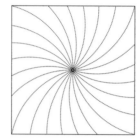
Starburst with Curves

There is movement in both designs created by the radiation of the lines from the center, but the straight lines feel strong and static while the curved lines create soft, flowing movement and lightness. Diagonal lines carry an inherent sense of movement while vertical and horizontal lines are more stable. Consider curves or diagonals when movement is important in your quilt.

When looking at Swing (opposite), I hope you can see that it is all about movement. The quilting supports the movement and the action of a pendulum. The quilting lines begin at a deep angle in the upper right and the angle lessens as the lines progress across the quilt and terminate at the vertical left edge. The diagonal lines imply movement and action which is perfect for this quilt.

146

TAKE ADVANTAGE OF THE PIECED STRUCTURE

The piecing of a quilt may be the best clue to the mystery of choosing a quilting design. Pay attention to your quilt's structure. Is there a grid, a set of shapes, or sections created by the piecing that could inform your quilting decision? Quilts made up of shapes with 60° angles are perfect candidates for those 60° Designs (see page 28). Does the piecing create a grid that can serve as the foundation for grid-based designs? The shapes you piece into your quilt can also be the impetus for a quilting design as in the Quiet Geometry quilt on page 140, where I used Rotational Designs to reinforce the circular piecing. Simillarly, in the Jay's Star quilt on page 144 where I used the seven sections created by the points of the star as the basis for the quilting. The piecing of our quilts creates the primary design element of the composition of a quilt, so look to that to find inspiration for your quilting design.

Spare a Square (opposite) is a simple charm square quilt pieced with 5″ squares. Since all the pieces in the quilt are the same size, it was a perfect candidate for a grid-based design. I quilted the Flower in Orange Peel design (see page 110). The pieced squares act as the base grid which make the quilting quick and easy since I didn't need to quilt the grid itself, only the curved parts of the design. The repeated grid-based design supports the regularity of the piecing and adds a motif that stands up to and complements the bold prints in the squares.

CREATE A MOOD OR FEELING

Some quilts call for quilting that helps create a mood or feeling for the quilt. Yoshiko's Cross is a special quilt honoring quilt artist Yoshiko Jinzenji and is the first quilt in which I considered what mood or feeling I wanted a quilt to have and how the quilting could be used to accomplish that vision. I wanted the quilt to have a contemplative, Japanese feel and the Sashiko inspired quilting created a quiet, meditative, and interesting background texture. Sometimes quilts need an infusion of personality and the quilting can do that job.

Quilts can feel gentle, exciting, serious or even whimsical and fun.

Whirlygig (opposite) is one of those quilts that called for a little whimsy. I quilted Whirlygig with three sets of Concentric Circles with Rotational Designs in the center of each of the concentrics. The circular quilting mimics the movement of pinwheels. The intricate rotational designs create multiple focal points which draw the viewer in and through the design. The quilting supports a fun, spirited quilt.

150

151

DISAPPEAR OR STABILIZE

Sometimes the quilting isn't necessary as a visual element at all. In some quilts the piecing needs to stand alone, and the quilting takes a back seat or plays a supporting role. One of my students shared a miniature log cabin quilt and asked for quilting advice. We were enthralled by her exquisite work and the piecing of those teeny tiny logs. The group came to the conclusion that she should stitch in the ditch around the blocks and that would be enough. Quilting-in-the-ditch hides the quilting and stabilizes and supports the pieced design, so that the piecing is the star of the show. Veer (opposite) is another example in which the majority of the quilting takes a back seat.

In Veer, quilting transforms a plain blue rectangle into a field of stars. The crosshatched lines are quilted with a larger interval to create a star-like motif. I used a heavier weight thread to make that quilting stand out. The remainder of the quilting fades away. The stripes of the flag and the background are quilted following the direction of the stripes with thread that matches the fabric, so that the quilting creates a barely visible, subtle texture that allows the striking design to take center stage. It doesn't always have to be fancy to be effective quilting.

A CAUTIONARY TALE

While quilting can make a major positive impact on the overall composition of a quilt, it can also interfere, compete with or overwhelm the design. The best example I have of quilting coming close to ruining a design before moving on to an almost-perfect partnership between piecing and quilting, is Running Man (opposite).

Running Man is pieced with narrow vertical strips, so I thought vertical matchstick quilting would be the perfect design. After quilting about a third of it, I hung it on the design wall to take a look. I knew right away I had made a terrible mistake. This quilt is all about the joy of movement and the runner simply stood still with those straight vertical lines repeated over and over. I spent some quality time with my seam ripper and tried again. I needed a design that emphasized movement. I chose sectioned curves and used the piecing to inform the placement of the curves. I set the first curve based on the runner's front leg and the second curve based on the back leg. I echoed each of those curves to fill in the two sections defined by the curves. The quilting transformed the quilt by creating a wonderful sense of movement and flow that is a perfect complement to the pieced design. I learned a lesson from Running Man and eventually it led to the set of questions on page 164 that I use with every quilt I make.

THERE ARE NO QUILTING SOUL MATES

While I think the quilting and piecing of Running Man is a pretty darn good marriage, sectioned curves is not the only quilting design that would have accomplished the goal of adding movement and making the runner come alive. There are no quilting soul mates. We don't have to search for the elusive one perfect quilting design for our quilt. There are always several quilting options available for every quilt that will create an effective composition. For example, Bricks (shown below) is a simple rectangular design mocked-up with four different quilting designs.

The first possibility emphasizes the pieced design with lines quilted in different directions in each section. The color and/or fabric differences define each section. This design is challenging since it requires turning, traveling and many stops and starts. The second

possibility uses a simple chevron to add dimension to the individual bricks. This design is moderately challenging because it requires large angle pivoting and minimal marking. The third option is the Arrow design (see page 53). This design creates new shapes and adds complexity to the quilt. The Arrow design is a bit simpler with vertical echoed lines and a slight angle pivot with minimal marking. Bricks is shown with simple horizontal channel quilting. This design is the easiest to execute but in its simplicity lets the pieced design shine through. Each quilting design requires different skills, time commitments and brings new elements to the quilt, and they are all good partners for the pieced design. We each have different situations, skill levels and restrictions that we work under for each quilt. Let's look at those considerations and how they affect the designs we choose.

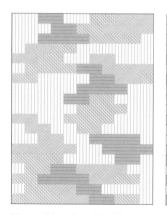

Linear Directional Quilting

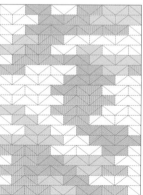

Linear Chevron Quilting

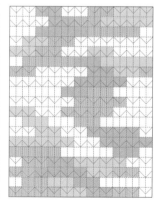

Arrow Quilting

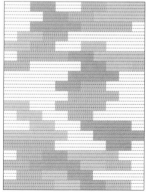

Horizontal Channel Quilting

CONSIDERATIONS AND RESTRICTIONS

As you contemplate what you desire for your next quilt, consider what you like, what restrictions you are operating under, your level of skill and experience with a design, and the number of options you have to choose from. Each of these considerations will influence your choice of a quilting design.

What Do I Like?

The first and for me the most important consideration is, what kind of quilting do I like? I love lines. I love simple. Once I figured out that linear, simple quilting was my 'go to' quilting, I stopped practicing swirly free motion things and concentrated on becoming a proficient walking foot quilter and filling my toolbox with designs that work for me. I love the quilting to support my piecing. I typically choose an overall design for my quilt. I love small intervals between lines. I'm a matchstick quilting devotee. I also know what I don't like. Ask yourself what do you love? What thrills you when you see it on a quilt? What is your aesthetic preference? What would you never quilt on a quilt? The first step to knowing what you desire is figuring out what kinds of quilting you like on your quilts and then practicing and filling your quilting design toolbox with options that fit your likes.

Acknowledge and Work With Your Limitations

Having decided what you like in terms of quilting designs, we have to remember that we don't always get what we want. As quilters we operate under different circumstances and restrictions. We have different spaces, set-ups and different sewing machines. We need to acknowledge our restrictions and work with them and around them. We are restricted by the size of the harp on our machine and the amount of support we have built-in around it. If you have a sewing machine with a very small harp space, you probably don't want to choose a design that requires massive amounts of manipulation and turning. However, don't let restrictions derail you. Focus on what you can do with what you have or figure out a new way to do something. Learning the tips and tricks to handle large quilts and how to set up your space to support your quilt, can minimize the impact of your restrictions. Also remember that as you become more experienced and confident, you will be able to tackle more challenging designs on larger quilts.

OVERCOMING LIMITATIONS

Angela Walters quilted Add It Up (below) on her longarm and she used the design I call Tower of Triangles from *WALK* on parts of it. I loved that design and I wanted to use it on other quilts. At the time, I wasn't proficient in free-motion quilting like Angela. The design is composed of simple lines so I gave it a go with my walking foot. The small harp on my machine made the turning required to execute that design a limitation I couldn't overcome. Years later when I was experimenting with quilting in reverse, I tried the design again and lo and behold, it worked and was super-simple to execute. Moral of the story: think out of the box to find a way.

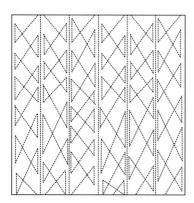

Tower of Triangles

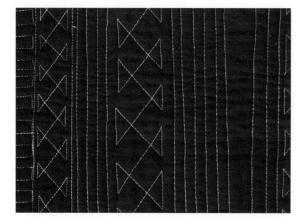

Size Matters

The size of your quilt makes a difference as you consider quilting design options. Some designs are much more challenging on larger quilts. I recommend that the first time you execute a design, quilt it on a smaller piece like a pillow, table runner or even a baby quilt and then move up to larger pieces. Practicing with a quilting design on smaller pieces builds muscle memory, skill and most importantly, confidence. I remember quilting my first spiral on a baby quilt. I was petrified and the spiral was a little wobbly and took what seemed like forever, but I did it. After countless spirals on all sizes of quilts, spiraling has now become easy for me. The designs in the Rotational Designs chapte are new to me and I've quilted all of them on 18″ × 18″ samples to learn the technique and build my confidence. Practice is magical, but remember it doesn't need to be perfect. It only needs to be the best you can do that day. Each quilting design option requires different skills and amounts of manipulation and quilt turning. A good way to know if you can handle the quilt and the chosen design is to do a dry run with the quilt and your machine. Place your quilt in the harp and simulate and practice the movements required by the design you chose. Turn the quilt and even stitch without the machine threaded to see what you can handle. You might surprise yourself. You might even decide that it's not going to happen. I always do a dry run when I'm tackling a challenging design for the first time, especially on a larger quilt.

Adapt

Some designs can be modified to make them much easier to quilt on small machines or simply easier to quilt in general and still give close to the same effect as the more complex version. For many of the designs in this book I offer specific ideas to modify the design for simpler quilting. Here are a few general strategies you might employ to scale down the difficulty of a design.

REDUCE THE ANGLE OF THE PIVOT

The steeper the angle required when pivoting, the more difficult the design will become, because the quilt needs to be turned more. Look at the two versions of Sashiko Cubes below. Notice the steep angle in version one compared to the gentler angle in version two. The latter will be much easier to quilt.

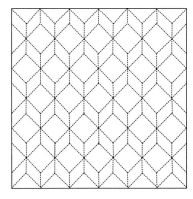

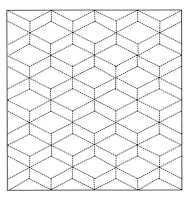

Sashiko Cubes

REDUCE THE DEPTH OF A CURVE

The same principle applies with curves as it does with pivoting. The gentler the curve, the easier it is to quilt because the quilt doesn't have to move as much. Windsails on page 60 and Wings page 66 are similar designs. They both have a beautiful flow and movement, but Windsails is much easier to quilt because the curves are very slight and the pivot is small. The Wings design has deeper curves and a much steeper pivot, which makes it a much more challenging design. If the instructions call for marking a ½″ depth of a curve, change the marking to ¼″ to reduce the difficulty.

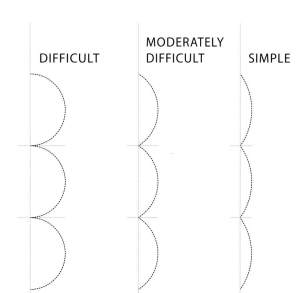

Three Different Markings for Curves

REDUCE THE NUMBER OF TURNS REQUIRED

The number of turns required by a design also increases its difficulty. The quilting is divided into four squares sections. The sections are echoed in with multiple turns required for each round of quilting in each section. The same area is divided into the same four sections but the echo quilting only requires one turn for each round. This makes the design much easier to quilt and they look very similar.

SUPERSIZE THE DESIGN

Supersizing a design reduces its difficulty by enabling you to quilt the design once rather than multiple times. The design will also be easier to quilt because it will require gentler curves or shallower pivots and there is less quilt to move through the harp. It is much easier to quilt one Rose Spiral (see page 127) starting in the center of the quilt and radiating out to the edges, than it is to quilt the design in each block. The wobbles in the spiral are smaller and more challenging to quilt when they are executed in a single block. In Geared Up (right) I repeated the Geometric Curves design four times, one in each block. To make it even easier on myself, I could have quilted a supersized version of the design on the entire quilt.

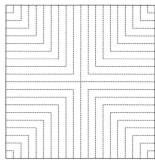

Quilting with Multiple Turns   *Quilting with One Turn*

160

INCREASE THE INTERVAL BETWEEN LINES

The interval you choose between lines, the size of the grid you choose to quilt when crosshatching, or the number of lines in a design, all affect the level of difficulty of the quilting. Including more lines, increases the time it takes to quilt. Pinwheels (see page 38) and Flowers in Circles (see page 42) are 60° designs. These are great examples of using fewer lines to reduce the difficulty, while maintaining a similar look and feel to the design. Both are based on the same Equilateral Triangle Grid and are quilted with the same technique. The Flowers in Circles design requires many more lines of quilting and the deeper curves result in a more challenging and time-consuming design.

CREATE SECTIONS

Another way to reduce difficulty is to create sections within a quilt or by combining shapes or blocks to define areas for quilting. Look at Division (right). Most of the triangles in this example are quilted with different quilting designs. Notice, however, that three of the lightest triangles are combined and are quilted with one design. I made it easier on myself by quilting the Geometric Curves design in that combined area rather than in a single triangle. As you are considering how to quilt a quilt, think about how blocks, shapes, or areas of the quilt can be combined to define quilting areas. The larger the area of a design the easier it will be to quilt.

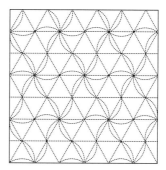
Pinwheels

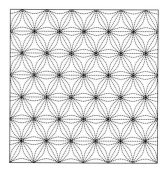
Flowers in Circles

161

QUILT AS-YOU-GO

Some quilts are giants. They are heavy. They are unwieldy. They are a bear to quilt on a home machine, but they can be done. Choosing simple designs for these quilts is typically a good idea if you are doing it yourself on your home machine. Sometimes the size of the quilt doesn't match your desired quilting and that is where the quilt-as-you-go technique may help.

Shape Study is 90″ square (see page 132). I wanted lines in each section to go in different directions but I wanted to minimize turning that big quilt many times. Also, I didn't want to compromise on the density. Quilt as-you-go allowed me to quilt each of the four sections which were a manageable size of 45″ square, one at a time. Then I put the four sections together as a whole quilt. If you're making one of these monsters, think about how the quilt could be divided into smaller sections and try quilt as-you-go. I highly recommend Marianne Haak's site *The Quilting Edge* (see page 175). She has been using the quilt as-you-go method for many years and has several excellent tutorials to help you learn how to do it yourself.

Time is Precious

Quilting is an investment of time and effort and time is a limited resource. There is never enough time to make everything we want to make. If it needs to be done tomorrow, trust me, don't choose matchstick quilting. The intricacy of the design, the amount of marking and the closeness of the interval between the lines will all add to the amount of time it will take to quilt your quilt. Sometimes what we desire is fast and easy.

Fill Your Quilting Design Toolbox

The final consideration is how many designs do I have in my quilting design toolbox? It's all about options. I want to be able to look at a quilt top and have multiple options come to mind. *WALK* and *WALK 2.0* are filled with options for you: lines, curves, textures, and so much more. Stephanie Yu-Falkenstein (see page 175) is a great role model as a quilter who has filled her toolbox and I recommend that you follow her lead. Stephanie made small sample sandwiches and stitched out many of the designs from *WALK*. She built her confidence one design at a time and now has loads of designs to choose from when she is faced with quilt as desired. Stephanie knows that quilting doesn't just happen; it takes effort, practice with a bit of determination and a sense of humor thrown in. Her vintage BERNINA isn't going to magically grow a large harp, but because of her effort she knows she has options that look great and that are achievable on the equipment she owns. Check out her Instagram feed or the hashtag #WALKBOOK to be inspired.

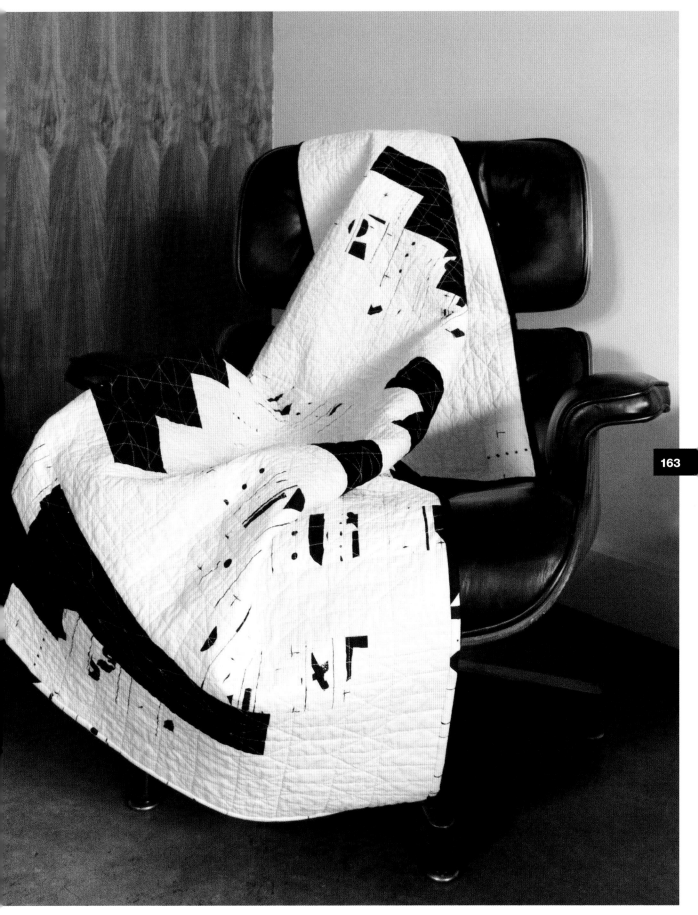

QUILT AS DESIRED – THE PROCESS

The Process

→ **Question 1** What is important about this quilt?

→ **Question 2** What does this quilt need?

→ **Question 3** What can I do?

With the information and experience gained from teaching and quilting, I've developed a process that helps me answer the question, how do I quilt my quilt? The process is a set of three questions that I ask myself to help me determine a quilting design. I typically do this in my studio sitting in my orange chair looking at the quilt top and I talk out loud to myself. It is even better to do this process with friends or family because they will bring another perspective to the piece and will ask you more questions to spark ideas.

Q1 / WHAT IS IMPORTANT ABOUT THIS QUILT?

The first question in my evaluation is actually something Angela Walters asked me. In working with Angela as a beginning quilter, I would show her my quilt and she would ask me, "What is important about this quilt?" This question sparked me to think and talk about my quilt and from that conversation, an idea would almost always emerge. This question encourages you to think about why you made the quilt, what you love about it, or what stands out to you. Quilters have answered this question by pointing out a certain fabric they love, being proud of the piecing, or talking about the inspiration for the quilt or even the person they made it for. Sometimes the answer is simply, "It's important that it get done!" but often, if you can have that conversation with yourself, a plan will reveal itself to you.

Q2 / WHAT DOES THIS QUILT NEED?

The next question, "What does this quilt need?" is designed to encourage you to look closely at your quilt. Look at the design, the shapes, the directionality, the type of symmetry, the structure, the focal point, and the fabrics. Are there defined sections or could they be created with quilting? Is there something missing that quilting could add like a focal point? Is there something the quilting could emphasize?

Q3 / WHAT CAN I DO?

As you generate options, the third question comes into play. What can I do? Do I want to try something I've never done before? Which of my options is realistic and achievable? What do I need to do to make this happen? At this point in the process, consider your options. Draw your ideas on a photo of your quilt using a graphics program or go old school and use an acetate cover so you can erase one design and try another.

Another option is use a Hera marker and "draw" the creases onto the quilt top to test out how a design might look.

A quick ironing "erases" the creases and you can try again.

Tip: If you've never used a Hera marker, it's like a bone folder, a hard plastic tool with a point on one end and a curve on the other. Use it to "mark" creases on your quilt.

Put your options up and compare them. Think on it for a day or two if you need to, then make a decision and execute. Have fun and enjoy the process. It's going to be great!

DESIGN PARALYSIS

My last bit of advice is to avoid quilting design paralysis which occurs when you stumble into that pitfall of trying to find the perfect fit for a quilt or the quilt is so special that you're afraid to quilt it. I've been there. I had a quilt in my closet that was extremely challenging to make, and that I was so proud of that I was afraid to quilt it. I told myself over and over that it needed something special and I hadn't found the "right" design to make it sing. I even worked with several longarm quilters and I wasn't satisfied with their ideas either. It hung in the closet languishing for over five years. It's quilted now and I'm thrilled with it. I kick myself a bit for waiting so long. It's not perfect, but it is out in the world being used and I'm totally proud of it.

IMPLEMENTING THE PROCESS

Flower Power is a fun, whimsical quilt with a 70's vibe. Let's walk through the process with this quilt.

1. What is important about this quilt is how special my friend is to me and I want the quilt to reflect her personality. She's fun and happy and loves flowery, girly things.

2. What do I think this quilt needs? The flowers in this quilt are full of movement since they are made of circles and the block design radiates out from the center. I wanted to reinforce that movement so a curvy design would be a must. I came up with four curved options: rotational arcs, an echoed gentle curve, concentric circles, and the flowers in circles. It is important to me to have options to choose from. I mocked up these designs on the computer so I could see them. Auditioning designs on the quilt top helped me make my choice before I had to commit.

Arcs

Echo Curves

Concentric Circles

3. What can I do? I can handle all of these quilting options, but as always, this is a last-minute deal. I needed something I could accomplish pretty quickly, so I decided to eliminate the Flowers in Circles design because it would have been the most time consuming. While I liked Concentric Circles, it looked too safe and regular on this quilt and so did the echoes. After looking at Concentric Circles, I thought it might look better on each flower rather than one centered set of circles.

It was better, but still not quite right. As you consider your options and talk them through, one idea can lead to others. I then thought about the Spiral and the Rose Spiral variation.

This design is more fun and a bit goofy and I like it better for this quilt. The Arcs (see page 79) and the Rose Spiral (see page 127) done on each block were definitely my favorites and ultimately I chose the arcs. The arcs add so much movement and I like how they move the eye from the center outwards. Even though they require a lot of marking, they are pretty quick to quilt and my friend is so worth an investment of time. In the end I had six design ideas to choose from that would all have been lovely on this quilt. You may have chosen a different design or come up with something totally different. The goal is for the process to lead you to a decision that you can execute, so that the quilt gets done, home with its intended owner and not hanging in your closet waiting for that perfect quilting.

Flowers in Circles

Concentric Circles

Rose Sprial

TECHNICAL CONSIDERATIONS

While the design of the quilting is important, thread color and thread weight choices make a significant difference in the quality of the stitches and the look of the quilt after the quilt is quilted.

Thread

Thread color as well as thread type and weight need to be considered before you begin the quilting process. The trick to thread selection is to choose the correct type, weight (thickness), color and fiber to achieve the look you desire. I have been a conservative thread user for many years, but no longer. I encourage you to be adventurous too. I'm a newbie thread explorer and haven't been out of my thread comfort zone for very long, but there is a wild, wonderful world of threads out there for quilters to explore. Let's do it!

Choosing thread for quilting begins with both knowing the basics and the options that are available. Take your time and investigate different types of thread. The more you try, the more you will learn.

THREAD WEIGHT

Typically, quilters use quilting thread. Quilting thread can be cotton, polyester or a blend and the fiber you choose is mostly a matter of personal preference. Quilting thread undergoes several processes to increase its strength, color, longevity and to reduce its lint production. For me, all of these make it a better choice than all-purpose thread. Quilting thread comes in a variety of thread weights. Higher numbered threads are thinner while lower number threads are thicker. For example, 80-weight is very fine thread while 12-weight is thick and hefty. Thicker threads will have more "presence" on the quilt. The samples for *WALK 2.0* were quilted with 28-weight thread so that the stitches show well and the quilting designs can be seen easily. I increase the stitch length (3.0) with thicker threads to give the stitches space to form. In my machine, I used 28-weight thread in both the top and the bobbin. Heavier weight thread is a bold choice. I quilted Mid-Century House (shown here on the right) with 28-weight, turquoise thread with a complex grid. The piecing is high contrast so it could stand up to the high impact quilting to form a powerful composition. The samples in the book are also quilted with 28-weight white thread so the quilting stitches are well defined and bold on the black background.

With very thick 12-weight thread, I use a 40-weight thread in the bobbin. I've found through experimentation that this is the best combination to get good stitch quality with my machine. You may need to do some test stitching to find the right combination and tension settings with your machine. If I want the quilting stitches to blend more and sink into the quilt I use a lighter weight thread, typically 50-weight. I have a few

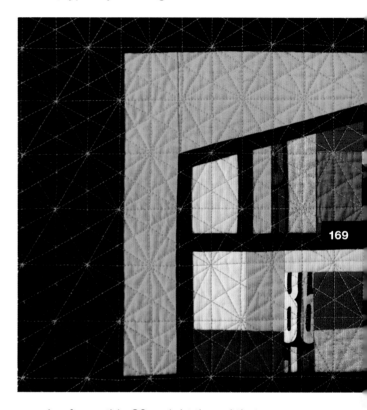

169

spools of very thin 80-weight thread that I use for stitching-in-the-ditch. This very fine thread hides well in the ditch and even when I wander out a bit the stitches tend to disappear. Don't be afraid to combine multiple thread weights in one quilt as I did in Argyle (see page 35). You may want the quilting to stand out in some areas and blend or fall back in other areas as I did in Veer (see page 152). I used 28-weight thread for the stars and 50-weight thread for the remainder of the quilting.

THREAD COLOR

Which color thread do you typically choose when quilting? Do you like to match thread to each color of fabric in your quilt? Do you like to find a thread that blends with all of the colors in your quilt? Are you an, "I-will-use-beige-thread-and-it-will-be-all-good" kind of person? All of those are good choices, but thread color makes a difference in your quilting plan. Matching thread color to fabrics makes the quilting subtler and less impactful. Combining a contrasting color with a lighter weight thread, lessens the impact of the color as well, but still adds interest and life. The higher the contrast between the quilting thread and the quilt and the heavier the weight of the thread, the more prominent your quilting will be.

I used four colors of 50-weight thread on the Honey's Moons quilt that match each of the moon colors. I love how the quilt shimmers a bit with the different colored threads and how folks are surprised when they see the colors. With every quilt, I audition thread colors by laying or pooling lengths of thread onto the quilt top. There are several colors that act as chameleons and seem to take on the color of the fabric on which they appear. One of those is Aurifil #2524. It is a purplish gray and blends beautifully across many colors. You don't know how a color will look unless you try it. If the background of your quilt is light, try colors like light peach, butter yellow, light pink or a very light blue instead of white. They can add a little twinkle to your quilting without being too much. It can be interesting in an overall design to use multiple colors of thread

171

in the same design. Argyle (see page 35) is designed to be quilted in multiple colors. So what to do on a high contrast quilt (like a black and white one)? Maybe you want to do a design with one thread color? In this case, density is important. If you quilt one or two lines of white thread a few inches apart down the center of a black fabric, the thread will be vivid against the dark background. The impact of high contrast thread is minimized when there are more lines of quilting at a small interval. With small intervals the lines merge and create more of a screen-like look rather than prominent lines. For me, lines start to merge at a ½″ interval or less. Any farther than that, they tend to read more as separate lines.

SEND OFF

"Quilt as Desired" will always be a bit intimidating as we finish our tops and face that statement. Understanding more about how quilting adds to the design of a quilt and the principles underlying those design options, helps us respond to that statement with knowledge and confidence. Armed with the information, example quilts and the process in this section, it is time to face the music and answer the question, "How do I quilt my quilt?" I know you can do it.

TIPS FOR HANDLING LARGE QUILTS

1. Place support for your quilt behind and to the left of your machine with tables or ironing boards added around your sewing table.

2. If possible, sink your machine into the table so it is flush with the tabletop.

3. Scrunch or accordion-fold your quilt rather than rolling it. Scrunching and accordion folding compresses the quilt to get it through the harp but allows you the flexibility to handle and manipulate it in front of the machine. A rolled quilt is an inflexible log.

4. Use your chest to support the section of quilt you're working on and let the remainder pool in your lap or rest on the table to your left. Stop and pull up more quilt onto your chest as you quilt.

5. Consider your hand position as you quilt. Sometimes flat hands on the quilt make it easier to guide. With some designs I use a flat left hand and I grip the quilt with my right hand. This is especially effective with gently curved designs.

6. Wear quilting gloves (see page 175) or use other aids that will help you grip and move your quilt.

7. A Supreme Slider (see page 175) keeps the bed of your machine slippery so that the quilt moves more easily through the harp. Cut an opening in the slider so that the feed dogs are revealed and can do their work with the walking foot.

FINAL SEND OFF: It has been quite a journey writing this book. I wondered from the beginning if I was pushing the walking foot too far. Would quilters even want more walking foot designs? I was lifted up, encouraged and inspired by the students in my walking foot classes to push the envelope and keep on sharing. My hope is that with *WALK 2.0* you will increase your skill with the walking foot, build your confidence, find new designs to enhance your quilts and have a process to create a quilting plan for each quilt you make. Quilt on!

INTERVAL TOOLS

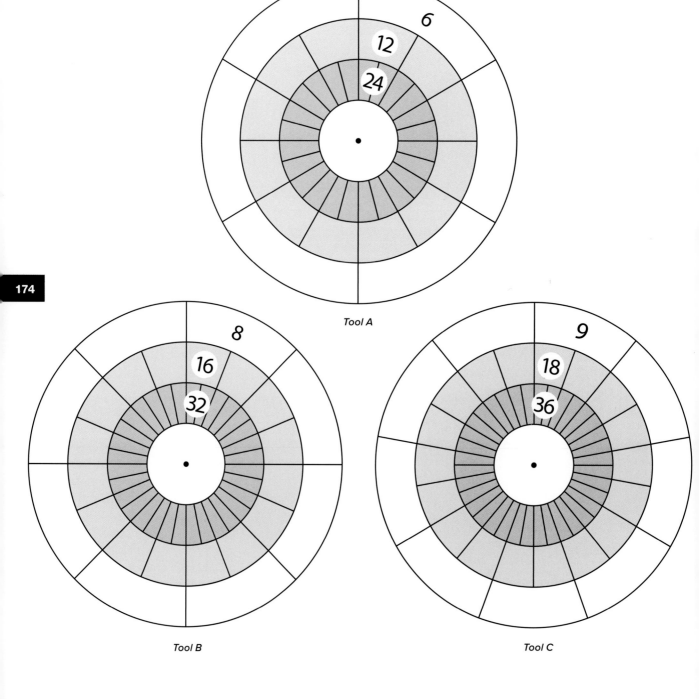

6

12

24

Tool A

8

16

32

Tool B

9

18

36

Tool C

RESOURCES

MARKING TOOLS

Sewline Ceramic Pencil Product Information

Available at many local quilt shops or on Amazon.com

Sewline.com.au/product/fabric-pencil

Pen-Style Chaco Liners, Clover HERA Marker, Clover Water

Soluble Markers
clover-usa.com

Carpenter's Compass

Simple compass for drawing all sizes of circles

Homedepot.com

Anita Shackelford's Marking Templates

Perfect Spiral Tool

Anitashackelford.net/quilting_templates

Quilter's Rule Int'l

817 Mohr Avenue
Waterford, WI 53185
Quiltersrule.com

Marking tools and marking pencil remover

Nested circles 1″ to 12″ for marking circles and arcs

Comic Book Boards for Making Stencils

Amazon.com

Hancy's Ultimate Iron Off Marking Pencil

Fulllinestencil.com

Hancy's Quilt Pounce Iron Off Powder and Pounce Pad

Fulllinestencil.com

Pat Campbell White Marking Pencils

Patcampbell.com

Dritz Water Soluble Markers

Dritz.com

BASTING Supplies

Niagra spray starch
Niagarastarch.com

505 Spray and Fix Temporary Fabric Adhesive
odifusa.com

QUILTING and Finishing SUPPORT

Stephanie Yu-Falkenstein
Instagram: @sewbespokeandco

QAYG (quilt-as-you-go)

Marianne Haak and The Quilting Edge
thequiltingedge.com

Machingers Quilting Gloves

Available at many local quilt shops or Amazon

The Supreme Slider

Available at many local quilt shops or on Amazon

Side Threading Needles and Spiral Eye Needles

Theneedlelady.com

Superior Thread Thread Holder

Superiorthreads.com

Needle Type and Size Information

Schmetzneedles.com

Needle Size/Thread Weight Match

Weallsew.com

Superiorthreads.com

ACKNOWLEDGEMENTS

WALK 2.0 came from years of working with students who are as excited about their walking foot as I am. You motivated me to push myself and push the limits of the walking foot. As always, I learn as much from you as you do from me. Many of you have shared ideas for the content of this book and I am so grateful to have you as co-contributors! It is my hope that with *WALK 2.0* your quilting design toolbox will be overflowing and quilting your own quilts will be a smoother, more enjoyable process than ever.

The team at Lucky Spool is unsurpassed as creatives and collaborators and I am proud to be a member of the team that created this book. I admire and appreciate Kristy's style and design prowess and Kari's ability to interpret my crude work and turn it into beautiful, clear illustrations. Lauren, again we make a fabulous team. I'm so fortunate to be your partner in photography and styling. I love that we have fun working together and again you have made my work come alive with your mad skills. Shea, you work behind the scenes making sure everything says what I mean it to say in a concise, straightforward way and I can't thank you enough for making sure the book is technically sound. Laurena, thanks for braving 90° heat and sticky fingers to cut and baste all the sample sandwiches for the book. Susanne, I am proud to be a member of the Lucky Spool family and work with such an inspiring, dedicated and talented leader. I cherish our friendship and couldn't be prouder of the work we have done together.

Most importantly I have a rock-solid support system that makes long days and nights of writing and creating possible. Mom, I love you and love that you support me 100%. Ben, Jon, Courtney and Karissa, I appreciate your cheering me on every step of the way. Your positive comments and enthusiasm for my work mean so much to me. Buzz, you are my partner and together we are still on a roll.